Blueprints Q&A
STEP 2: PEDIATRICS

Blueprints Q&A
STEP 2: PEDIATRICS

SERIES EDITOR:
Michael S. Clement, MD

Fellow, American Academy of Pediatrics
Mountain Park Health Center
Phoenix, Arizona
Clinical Lecturer in Family
   and Community Medicine
University of Arizona College of Medicine
Consultant, Arizona Department
   of Health Services

EDITOR:
Janice P. Piatt, MD

Associate Director, Pediatric Clinic
Medical Director, Bill Hold Pediatric HIV Clinic
Phoenix Children's Hospital
   Phoenix, Arizona

**Blackwell
Science**

©2002 by Blackwell Science, Inc.

EDITORIAL OFFICES:

Commerce Place, 350 Main Street,
 Malden, Massachusetts 02148, USA

Osney Mead, Oxford OX2 0EL, England

25 John Street, London WC1N 2BL, England

23 Ainslie Place, Edinburgh EH3 6AJ, Scotland

54 University Street, Carlton, Victoria 3053, Australia

OTHER EDITORIAL OFFICES:

Blackwell Wissenschafts-Verlag GmbH,
 Kurfürstendamm 57, 10707 Berlin, Germany

Blackwell Science KK, MG Kodenmacho Building,
 7-10 Kodenmacho Nihombashi, Chuo-ku,
 Tokyo 104, Japan

Iowa State University Press, A Blackwell Science Company,
 2121 S. State Avenue, Ames, Iowa 50014-8300, USA

DISTRIBUTORS:

The Americas
> Blackwell Publishing
> c/o AIDC
> P.O. Box 20
> 50 Winter Sport Lane
> Williston, VT 05495-0020
> (Telephone orders: 800-216-2522;
> fax orders: 802-864-7626)

Australia Blackwell Science Pty, Ltd.
> 54 University Street
> Carlton, Victoria 3053
> (Telephone orders: 03-9347-0300;
> fax orders: 03-9349-3016)

Outside The Americas and Australia
> Blackwell Science, Ltd.
> c/o Marston Book Services, Ltd., P.O. Box 269
> Abingdon, Oxon OX14 4YN, England
> (Telephone orders: 44-01235-465500;
> fax orders: 44-01235-465555)

Acquisitions: Beverly Copland

Development: Angela Gagliano

Production: Irene Herlihy

Manufacturing: Lisa Flanagan

Marketing Manager: Toni Fournier

Cover design by Hannus Design

Typeset by Software Services

Printed and bound by Courier-Stoughton

Printed in the United States of America

01 02 03 04 5 4 3 2 1

The Blackwell Science logo is a trade mark of Blackwell Science Ltd., registered at the United Kingdom Trade Marks Registry

Library of Congress Cataloging-in-Publication Data

Blueprints Q & A step 2. Pediatrics / editor,
Janice P. Piatt.
  p. ; cm.—(Blueprints Q & A step 2 series)
 title: Pediatrics
 ISBN 0-632-04598-1 (pbk.)
 1. Pediatrics—Examinations, questions, etc.
 2. Physicians—Licenses—United States—Examinations—
Study guides. I. Title: Blueprints Q&A step 2. Pediatrics
II. Title: Pediatrics. III. Piatt, Janice P. IV. Series.
 [DNLM: 1. Pediatrics—Examination Questions. WS 18.2
B658 2002]
 RJ48.2.B58 2002
 618.92'00076—dc21   2001002524

Notice: The indications and dosages of all drugs in this book have been recommended in the medical literature and conform to the practices of the general community. The medications described and treatment prescriptions suggested do not necessarily have specific approval by the Food and Drug Administration for use in the diseases and dosages for which they are recommended. The package insert for each drug should be consulted for use and dosage as approved by the FDA. Because standards for usage change, it is advisable to keep abreast of revised recommendations, particularly those concerning new drugs.

CONTRIBUTORS:

Paul Bergeson, MD
Attending in Pediatrics
Phoenix Children's Hospital
Phoenix, Arizona

Vasudha L. Bhavaraju, MD
Resident in Pediatrics
Phoenix Children's Hospital and
    Maricopa Medical Center
Phoenix, Arizona

Randal C. Christensen, MD, MPH
Attending in Pediatrics
Phoenix Children's Hospital
Medical Student Clerkship Director
Good Samaritan Regional Medical Center
Phoenix, Arizona

Krista Lee Colletti, MD
Resident in Pediatrics
Phoenix Children's Hospital
Phoenix, Arizona

Veronica Heather Flood, MD
Resident in Pediatrics
Phoenix Children's Hospital
Phoenix, Arizona

Jeffrey Foti, MD
Resident in Pediatrics
Phoenix Children's Hospital and
    Maricopa Medical Center
Phoenix, Arizona

Theresa A. Grebe, MD
Attending in Pediatrics
Phoenix Children's Hospital
Phoenix, Arizona

John R. Hartley, DO
Resident
Phoenix Children's Hospital
Phoenix, Arizona

Donna L. Holland, MD
Attending in Pediatrics
Phoenix Children's Hospital
Phoenix, Arizona

Michelle B. Huddleston, MD
Attending in Pediatrics
Phoenix Children's Hospital
Phoenix, Arizona

Jennifer L. Matchey, MD
Resident
Phoenix Children's Hospital
Phoenix, Arizona

John Robert Muhm, Jr., MD
Attending in Pediatrics
Phoenix Children's Hospital
Phoenix, Arizona

Kay C. Pinckard, MD
Attending in Pediatrics
Phoenix Children's Hospital
Phoenix, Arizona

Lisa Sieczkowski, MD
Resident in Pediatrics
Phoenix Children's Hospital
Phoenix, Arizona

Kristin Struble, MD
Resident in Pediatrics
Phoenix Children's Hospital
Phoenix, Arizona

Kristin Truell, MD
Chief Resident in Pediatrics
Phoenix Children's Hospital
Phoenix, Arizona

Thomas J. Van Osdol, MD
Resident in Pediatrics
Phoenix Children's Hospital and
   Maricopa Medical Center
Phoenix, Arizona

Jennifer L. Wallace, MD
Resident
Phoenix Children's Hospital
Phoenix, Arizona

Michelle Wang, DO
Phoenix Children's Hospital
Phoenix, Arizona

Jeffrey Weiss, MD
Section Chief
Department of General Pediatrics
Phoenix Children's Hospital
Phoenix, Arizona

Kent C. Williams, MD
Phoenix Children's Hospital
Phoenix, Arizona

Cynthia Wong, MD
Resident in Pediatrics
Phoenix Children's Hospital
Phoenix, Arizona

REVIEWERS:

Joseph K. Lim, MD

Class of 1999

Northwestern University Medical School

Chicago, Illinois

Resident, Internal Medicine

Yale University School of Medicine

New Haven, Connecticut

Mark R. Mills, MD

Class of 2000

University of Mississippi Medical Center

Jackson, Mississippi

Resident, Department of Radiology

Baptist Memorial Hospital

Memphis, Tennessee

Jason Sluzevich, MD

Class of 2000

Yale University School of Medicine

New Haven, Connecticut

Resident, Department of Internal Medicine and
  Dermatology

University Hospital

Cincinnati, Ohio

PREFACE

The Blueprints Q&A Step 2 series has been developed to complement our core content Blueprints books. Each Blueprints Q&A Step 2 book (*Medicine, Pediatrics, Surgery, Psychiatry,* and *Obstetrics/Gynecology*) was written by residents seeking to provide fourth-year medical students with the highest quality of practice USMLE questions.

Each book covers a single discipline, allowing you to use them during both rotation exams as well as for review prior to Boards. For each book, 100 review questions are presented that cover content typical to the Step 2 USMLE. The questions are divided into two groups of 50 in order to simulate the length of one block of questions on the exam.

Answers are found at the end of each book, with the correct option screened. Accompanying the correct answer is a discussion of why the other options are incorrect. This allows for even the wrong answers to provide you with a valuable learning experience.

Blackwell has been fortunate to work with expert editors and residents—people like you who have studied for and passed the Boards. They sought to provide you with the very best practice prior to taking the Boards.

We welcome feedback and suggestions you may have about this book or any in the Blueprints series. Send to blue@blacksci.com.

All of the authors and staff at Blackwell wish you well on the Boards and in your medical future.

ACKNOWLEDGMENTS

We would like to extend our grateful thanks to Janice Raper for all of her hard work and assistance on this project.

BLOCK **ONE**

QUESTIONS

QUESTION 1

Which of the following patients with congenital heart disease would be expected to exhibit cyanosis?

A. A 2-year-old girl with tetralogy of Fallot and concomitant aplastic anemia with a hemoglobin concentration of 5 g/dl

B. A 6-year-old girl with Turner's syndrome and coarctation of the aorta

C. A term newborn with truncus arteriosus

D. An 18-month-old boy with a muscular VSD

E. A 10-year-old boy with a congenital ASD

QUESTION 2

A 3-year-old toddler with myelomeningocele was hospitalized for a community acquired pneumonia. After a routine urinary catheterization, the patient became tachypneic, tachycardic, wheezy, and hypotensive. What is the most likely etiology of this patient's state of shock?

A. Hypovolemic shock from dehydration

B. Septic shock from streptococcus pnemoniae bacteremia

C. Anaphylactic shock from latex allergy

D. Spinal shock from myelomengocele

E. Cardiogenic shock from obstructive cardiomyopathy

QUESTION 3

A baby presents to your office with a rash in the diaper area. The rash has 5–10 mm sized fragile blisters which break easily, leaving a red base crusting and a fine collarette of white skin. There is no history of fever or any other signs of systemic illness. Your choice of treatment would be:

A. Neosporin ointment

B. Mycolog cream

C. Bactroban ointment

D. Desitin

E. Amoxicillin orally

QUESTION 4

Neurological, intellectual, and physical development in infants and children occur in an orderly and sequential manner. All of the following are integers of developmental milestones EXCEPT:

A. Gross motor

B. Fine motor

C. Bone age

D. Language

E. Social

QUESTION 5

A 9-year-old girl presents to the emergency department. She appears acutely ill and complains of headache, nausea, vomiting, and abdominal pain. She appears moderately dehydrated. Which of the following does not support the diagnosis of diabetic ketoacidosis?

A. The presence of hyperpnea (Kussmaul's respiration) on exam

B. Low serum blood glucose

C. A history of polyuria, polydipsia, fatigue

D. Metabolic acidosis on laboratory examination

E. The presence of ketones in the urine

QUESTION 6

A 6-week-old male infant presents with a history of projectile vomiting for the past five days. Physical exam reveals a dehydrated, irritable, afebrile infant. Laboratory evaluation reveals hypochloremic, hypokalemic metabolic acidosis. The likely diagnosis is:

A. Normal reflux

B. Hypertrophic pyloric stenosis

C. Viral infection

D. Duodenal atresia

E. Hirschsprung's disease

QUESTION 7

An 8-year-old boy presents with a 2- to 3-day history of diarrhea, fever of 102–103°F, and vomiting. He is having stools more than 10 times daily. The stools are watery with tenesmus and flecked with gross blood. He is 5–6% dehydrated. The most likely diagnosis is:

A. Intussusception

B. Viral gastroenteritis

C. Shigella gastroenteritis

D. Ulcerative colitis

E. Meckel's diverticulum

QUESTION 8

A previously healthy 10-month-old child of Greek ancestry arrives in the emergency department with the acute onset of cough, fever, generalized jaundice, and tea-colored urine. Physical examination reveals scleral icterus, tachypnea, and crackles over the right lower lung field. The family history is significant for a maternal uncle who has been hospitalized for "anemia." This child's chest radiograph demonstrates right lower lobe pneumonia. The hemoglobin level is 6.2 gm/dl with a normal red cell size. Examination of the peripheral smear reveals red cell fragments and Heinz bodies are present. The etiology of this child's anemia is:

A. Iron deficiency

B. G6PD deficiency

C. Sickle cell disease

D. Thalassemia trait

E. Folate deficiency

QUESTION 9

A 34-year-old gravida 3 para 1 woman with Class D diabetes mellitus is 36 weeks pregnant. You appropriately refer her for a level II ultrasound. All of the following abnormalities may be seen EXCEPT:

A. Caudal regression syndrome

B. Large size for gestational age

C. Congenital heart defect

D. Omphalocele

E. Neural tube defects

QUESTION 10

A child is brought to you in the emergency room. He has a temperature of 103°F and respiratory distress. He is leaning forward and has a very anxious look. His voice is muffled, and he is unable to swallow. Roentgenogram shows a swollen epiglottis. Proper treatment at this time would include all of the following EXCEPT:

A. Oxygen therapy.

B. Have the child lie down on his back so that he can rest properly.

C. Reassure the child and allow the parent to hold him.

D. Notify an anesthesiologist and/or otolaryngologist.

E. Prepare for possible sudden pulmonary arrest.

QUESTION 11

A 2-year-old boy arrives comatose and unresponsive to the emergency department. The child has dried vomitus on his shirt and pants. The father indicates that he picked up the child from the grandmother's house 60 minutes ago. The grandmother said that she had dropped her medications on the floor and it was possible that the child ate some pills, but the father does not know the names of the medications. The most appropriate first step in the management of this child is which of the following?

A. Administer syrup of ipecac.

B. Send the father back to the grandmother's house to find out the names of the medicines.

C. Pass a large bore gastric tube and lavage the child's stomach.

D. Establish a secure airway.

E. Arrange for admission to the hospital ward to observe the neurological status carefully.

QUESTION 12

Which of the following is NOT true of Erb's palsy?

A. It affects the fourth and fifth cervical spinal nerves.

B. It can result from traction on the head, neck, and arms of large infants during a vaginal delivery.

C. The grasp reflex is intact.

D. The Moro, biceps, and radial reflexes are absent on the affected side.

E. The affected arm is adducted and internally rotated with the elbow extended, the forearm is in pronation, and the wrist is flexed.

QUESTION 13

A 2-year-old boy presents to the emergency department for evaluation following a witnessed seizure. The seizure was described as generalized, lasting less than 5 minutes with a short post-ictal period. The child has no history of seizures, no family history of seizures, and no history of head injury. His exam currently is normal, except for a red, bulging right tympanic membrane and a temperature of 39°C. What is the most appropriate management for this patient?

A. He should be sent for an urgent CT scan of the head.

B. He should be given antibiotics and antipyretics and observed at home.

C. He should be admitted to the hospital and an EEG should be performed.

D. He should be started on phenobarbital and sent home.

E. A lumbar puncture and blood cultures should be obtained and anticonvulsants started in the hospital.

QUESTION 14

A 6-week-old baby presents to the office. His weight is still near birth weight. He had a normal birth and delivery and has not had any signs of infection or illness. The physical examination does not reveal any significant abnormalities except for his thin appearance. A diagnosis of failure to thrive is made. Which of the following is indicated?

A. Immediate hospitalization and extensive lab tests

B. Increasing the caloric content of formula and frequent weight measurements

C. Starting solid foods since formula isn't resulting in good growth

D. Report to child protective services and immediate placement in foster care

E. Switching formula to a different cow's milk-based formula

QUESTION 15

A 6-month-old child is hospitalized with multiple bruises. Child abuse is suspected. As part of her evaluation, an ophthalmology consult is obtained. Which of the following ocular findings is most consistent with child abuse?

A. Retinal hemorrhage

B. Conjunctivitis

C. Strabismus

D. Leukocoria

E. Dacryocystitis

QUESTION 16

You are seeing a 13-year-old female with a history of asthma and a seizure disorder who has recently developed acne. The mother is concerned that this may be due to one of her medications. Which of the following drugs is NOT associated with acne?

A. Corticosteroids

B. Danazol

C. Tegretol

D. Iodides

QUESTION 17

Which of the following is NOT a cause of apnea in infants?

A. Sepsis

B. Prematurity

C. Hyperglycemia

D. Severe hypoxemia

E. Intraventricular hemorrhage

QUESTION 18

Billy is a 9-year-old boy who comes to your office for a well-child checkup. He has been healthy and doing well in school, but Billy's mother is concerned about his bedwetting. He has never had a prolonged period of nighttime dryness, and Billy currently wets every night, about 2–3 hours after going to sleep. Billy's father had enuresis until age 10, but he outgrew the problem without any treatment. The mother has tried restricting fluids prior to bed, but this has not helped. What step in management would you do next?

A. Order a urine culture and a voiding cystourethrogram.

B. Counsel the mother that enuresis is a self-limited problem that requires no intervention.

C. Start oral medication, either imipramine or desmopressin.

D. Counsel Billy and his mother on the use of a buzzer alarm conditioning device.

E. Use negative reinforcement techniques to punish Billy when he has wet nights.

QUESTION 19

An 8-month-old child with known tetralogy of Fallot becomes agitated and develops cyanosis. Which of the following treatments is not appropriate for this "spell"?

A. Administration of crystalloid

B. Morphine sulfate

C. Neo-synephrine

D. Nitroglycerin

E. Placing the child in a knee to chest position

QUESTION 20

A 6-week-old infant was seen in the emergency department for a 1-week history of vomiting and diarrhea without fever. On exam the patient was tachycardic, normotensive, lethargic, with a sunken fontanelle, dry mucous membranes, and decreased skin turgor. Mom states that the baby's last weight was 4 kg at his 1-month well-child checkup, and there has been no urine output today. What is the initial fluid resuscitation of choice and what is the fluid deficit?

A. 1/4 NS, 200 cc

B. 1/2 NS, 200 cc

C. NS, 200 cc

D. NS, 400 cc

E. 3% NS, 400 cc

QUESTION 21

A 2-month-old infant has a red papular eruption over the face with flaking around the eyebrows, behind the ears, in the axillae and inguinal areas and scalp. Which two of the following are unlikely?

A. Infantile acne

B. Seborrhea

C. Cradle cap

D. Contact dermatitis

E. Dry skin

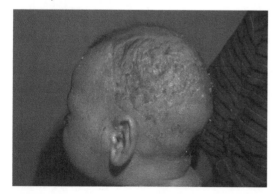

FIGURE 21

QUESTION 22

A 4-year-old boy is seen in the outpatient clinic for a yearly visit. His gross motor, visual motor, and social milestones are all appropriate. However, he uses only two word phrases, no pronouns, and knows about 50 words total. His language development is best described as:

A. Normal

B. A developmental delay

C. A developmental quotient

D. A developmental dissociation

E. A developmental deviancy

QUESTION 23

What is the immediate goal in the treatment of new onset insulin dependent diabetes mellitus (IDDM) and diabetic ketoacidosis (DKA)?

A. Start administration of dextrose intravenously.

B. Treat the acidosis with sodium bicarbonate.

C. Restore fluid and electrolyte losses and reverse the catabolic state.

D. Start antibiotics to treat any underlying infection that may have precipitated the DKA.

E. Screen the patient's siblings to see if they have IDDM also.

QUESTION 24

A 10-year-old child presents with a 1-month history of polydipsia, polyuria, and a 15 lb weight loss. All of the following will be seen upon further evaluation EXCEPT:

A. Dehydration

B. Kussmaul respirations

C. Metabolic alkalosis

D. Hyperglycemia

E. Glucosuria

QUESTION 25

A 12-month-old comes into the office with a 5-day history of diarrhea. Stools are soupy without water loss and no blood has been seen. Vomiting is intermittent. No fever has been noted. There is no history of foreign travel, but the child attends daycare. The most appropriate approach is:

A. Stool culture and sensitivity

B. Stool ova and parasites

C. Imodium orally or Lomotil orally

D. Trial of oral rehydration solution, increasing the diet gradually

E. Start antibiotics orally

QUESTION 26

For each of the following patients, match the corresponding blood test results:

1. A normal 2-month-old baby

2. An 18-month-old child who drinks an excessive amount of whole milk

3. A 2-year-old healthy, African-American child with alpha-thalassemia trait

4. A 15-month-old baby who drinks only goat's milk

5. A 7-year-old African-American child with sickle cell anemia

* MCV = mean corpuscular volume

** RDW = red cell distribution width (a measure of variation in size of red cells)

	Hemoglobin	MCV*	RDW**	Reticulocytes
A.	8.4 g/dl	high	high	low
B.	7.5	normal	high	very high
C.	9.9	very low	normal	normal
D.	5.0	low	high	low, normal
E.	8.5	normal	normal	normal

QUESTION 27

A young couple comes to your office for their first visit with their newborn daughter. Upon reviewing the hospital birth records, you note that the newborn screen is reported as abnormal for phenylketonuria (PKU). In counseling the parents about this diagnosis, all of the following are true statements EXCEPT:

A. The parents' recurrence risk is 25% in future pregnancies.

B. The child will need to be on a special formula restricting phenylalanine.

C. The prognosis for intellectual development is good with strict dietary management.

D. The dietary restriction may be discontinued when she is a teen.

E. Untreated patients develop mental retardation, spasticity, and behavior problems.

QUESTION 28

A 3-year-old is admitted to the hospital with a very pruritic rash. The infectious disease consultant identifies it as varicella (chickenpox). Which of the following is NOT true:

A. Varicella is highly contagious and this patient should be carefully isolated.

B. Varicella may be lethal in immunocompromised hosts.

C. Varicella is no longer contagious when all lesions are crusted over.

D. Varicella is pruritic to the extent that antipruritic drugs may be appropriate.

E. Varicella has an incubation period of only 5 days.

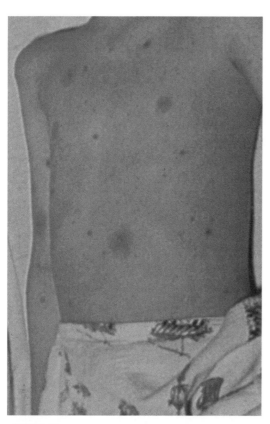

FIGURE 28

QUESTION 29

A 2-month-old baby girl is brought to your office for a routine visit. The baby is growing and developing well, and there are no medical problems. There were no problems with the pregnancy. Her mother tells you that her friend had a baby who recently died of sudden infant death syndrome (SIDS). Although there is no history of SIDS in her family, the mother is worried about her own child. You advise her to:

A. Use an apnea monitor (with a computer memory that is able to be downloaded for analysis).

B. Make sure the baby sleeps on her belly, to prevent aspiration if she vomits.

C. Put the baby to sleep on her back.

D. Make an appointment for a sleep study to rule out central and obstructive apnea.

E. Inform the mother that she should stop worrying since nothing she does can prevent SIDS.

QUESTION 30

A 3-day-old infant born at 27 weeks gestation in the NICU suddenly develops severe metabolic acidosis with abdominal distension. You suspect necrotizing enterocolitis (NEC). Which of the following signs or symptoms would you least likely see with necrotizing enterocolitis?

A. Ileus on abdominal x-ray

B. Temperature instability

C. Increased gastric aspirates (feeding residuals)

D. Oliguria

E. Non-bloody diarrhea

QUESTION 31

In which of the following conditions would you not expect to find an elevated alpha-fetoprotein level during a routine screen done at 16 weeks gestation?

A. Encephalocele

B. Myelomeningocele

C. Spina bifida

D. Subarachnoid hemorrhage

QUESTION 32

A 6-week-old male infant with a normal birth history has had poor weight gain. The mother reports that the infant cries inconsolably for hours at a time, frequently spits up his formula, and has had watery stools for the past 2 weeks. She had changed the formula at 1 month of age from cow-based formula to a soy-based formula because the baby was "colicky." The physical exam is significant for facial eczema, mild abdominal distention, and occult blood in the stool. Of the following, the most likely diagnosis is:

A. Lactose intolerance

B. Colic

C. Milk protein allergy

D. Gastroesophageal reflux

E. Necrotizing enterocolitis

QUESTION 33

While examining a 3-day-old infant born at term by NSVD to a 19-year-old primagravida mother without any perinatal infection or complications, you notice an asymmetric red reflex. The most common cause of this condition is:

A. Retinoblastoma

B. Congenital cataract

C. Retinopathy of prematurity

D. Congenital glaucoma

E. Ocular toxoplasmosis

QUESTION 34

An 11-year-old obese male presents with a significant limp for the past month. The pain began after a fall down the stairs at school. The pain is greatest in the anterior thigh and knee while walking. On examination, the leg is most comfortable in external rotation with some decrease in flexion in the knee and hip. Which of the following is correct?

A. Reassure the family that his pain will disappear when he grows out of his baby fat.

B. This is referred pain from a knee strain. Prescribe a knee brace and excuse him from physical education (PE).

C. Obtain x-rays of the hip.

D. Explain that the limp is due to extra weight on the pelvic bones and recommend a diet.

E. Make the parents aware that he is probably trying to avoid PE because he is overweight, resulting in teasing in the locker room.

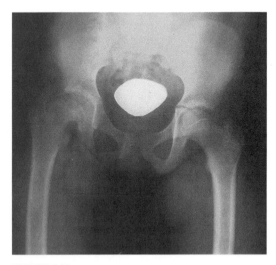

FIGURE 34A

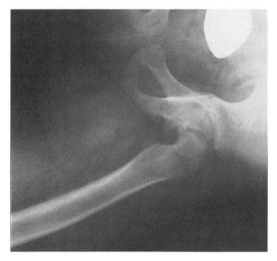

FIGURE 34B

QUESTION 35

An 8-year-old female with a history of reactive airway disease presents to your office for evaluation. She states that she uses her inhaled beta2-agonist 4–5 times a week. She takes no other medications. She was hospitalized once last winter for an asthma exacerbation, but has been well since. She has some limitations in her exercise tolerance secondary to shortness of breath. She denies any pets at home and there is no tobacco exposure. Which of the following medications should be added to her current regimen?

A. Antihistamine

B. Cromolyn sodium

C. Theophylline

D. Inhaled steroid

E. Daily prednisone

QUESTION 36

A 5-year-old boy develops the acute onset of testicular pain. There is no fever or history of trauma. You are considering both testicular torsion and orchitis. Which of the following is false?

A. The pain of orchitis is relieved by gently elevating the testicle.

B. Orchitis is more common in childhood than torsion.

C. Irreversible damage may occur as a result of testicular torsion.

D. When orchitis is diagnosed, antibiotics are normally unnecessary.

E. The incidence of orchitis has diminished since the introduction of the measles/mumps/rubella (MMR) vaccine.

QUESTION 37

You are conducting a well-child visit. The mother is concerned because a neighbor commented to her that she could only understand about half of what the 2-year-old boy was saying. The mother is wondering whether this is appropriate or whether she should be offended. You advise her:

A. This is appropriate for his age.

B. This is not appropriate for his age.

C. You reassure her but recommend speech therapy if she wants.

D. Arrange speech therapy immediately.

E. Refer the son to ear, nose, and throat (ENT) clinic.

QUESTION 38

An 11-year-old boy is seen in the emergency department for evaluation of symptoms of exertional dyspnea, chest pain, and cyanosis. He reports being previously healthy, but was told in the past that he had an "innocent" heart murmur. On exam, you detect a short holosystolic murmur, a right ventricular heave, and a loud pulmonary component of S2. The EKG demonstrates right ventricular hypertrophy, an increase in pulmonary vascularity. Cardiomegaly is seen on chest x-ray. What is the best explanation for this constellation of findings?

A. The patient has pathology in the pulmonary outflow tract leading to insufficient pulmonary blood flow.

B. The patient has an innocent flow murmur and needs no further evaluation.

C. The patient has evidence of Eisenmenger physiology.

D. The patient has coarctation of the aorta and secondary heart failure.

QUESTION 39

You are called to the bedside of a 1-month-old infant who is status post repair of coarctation of the aorta. He has been doing well and his feedings have been restarted. Since this morning, he has become more tachypneic. On exam, the patient has diminished breath sounds on the right with dullness to percussion. CXR shows a large effusion, so you urgently perform a diagnostic thoracentesis. The fluid returned is milky, and the patient continues to deteriorate. What is the most likely diagnosis?

A. Hemothorax from cardiac surgery

B. Parenteral nutrition leaking into the thoracic cavity

C. Chylothorax from thoracic duct injury during surgery

D. Parapneumonic effusion from a post-op pneumonia

E. Hydrothorax

QUESTION 40

A 4-year-old presents with a dry scaling rash which recurs intermittently. The family history is positive for asthma, allergy, and eczema. Treatment of eczema includes which of the following?

A. Keeping the skin scrupulously clean with baths twice daily

B. Allergy testing and allergy shots

C. A strict elimination diet

D. Steroid cream and moisturizing lotion

E. Prednisone (oral steroid)

QUESTION 41

In females, which of the following events signifies the onset of puberty?

A. Menarche

B. Growth spurt (height)

C. Pubic hair

D. Thelarche

E. Voice changes

QUESTION 42

A 7-year-old girl remains hospitalized following surgical removal of a craniopharyngioma. On post-operative day 1, she begins to have an increased volume of urine output. Which of the following would you also anticipate if no action is taken?

A. Low urine specific gravity

B. Low urine osmolality

C. Rise in serum sodium

D. Increase in hemoglobin

E. All of the above

QUESTION 43

A 3-year-old child is seen in the emergency department with a recent history of eating a fast food hamburger. The child has bloody diarrhea. Laboratory evaluation reveals anemia, thrombocytopenia, elevated BUN, and creatinine. Serum potassium is 8. Treatment should include all of the following EXCEPT:

A. 12 lead EKG

B. Admission to the pediatric intensive care unit

C. Calcium gluconate

D. Insulin and glucose

E. Aggressive fluid management (i.e., 2–3 times maintenance fluids)

QUESTION 44

A 10-year-old presents with a 1-year history of abdominal pain which is "always there," but waxes and wanes. She is an "A" student and competes on a state level in-figure skating. Mom describes her as a happy child who doesn't seem to be stressed. Most likely diagnosis:

A. Appendicitis

B. Parasitic enteritis

C. Inflammatory bowel disease (IBD)

D. Chronic abdominal pain

E. Gallbladder disease

QUESTION 45

A 6-year-old male presents with a 3-week history of leg pain which has increasingly worsened. He has spiking fevers at night, but no rashes. He now awakens at night crying with pain, and his mother is worried that he is fatigued and pale. Blood counts reveal a hemoglobin of 10.4 g/dl, platelet count of 85,000, and WBC is 28,000, with 80% lympths and 10% blast forms. A diagnosis of leukemia is made. Further testing is consistent with L2 morphology and is PAS negative. Unfavorable or high-risk prognostic factors in this case include all of the following EXCEPT:

A. Male sex

B. Age

C. Cell morphology

D. Platelet count

E. Hemoglobin

QUESTION 46

Which of the following statements is true regarding this patient's condition?

A. This condition is autosomal dominant.

B. This condition cannot be detected prenatally.

C. This condition is usually caused by a missing chromosome.

D. Affected individuals are usually females while males die in utero.

E. This condition has an extremely poor prognosis for survival past one month of age.

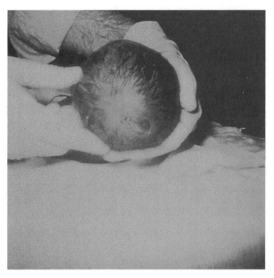

FIGURE 46B

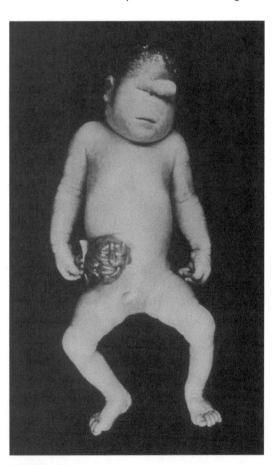

FIGURE 46A

QUESTION 47

A 10-year-old female presents to your office with a 4-day history of non-productive cough, low grade fever of 100.5°F, and now complains of a rash for one day. She has been taking an over-the-counter cough suppressant and Tylenol. She is otherwise healthy. On physical exam, she has a temperature of 99.9°F and a respiratory rate of 20. Her lung exam reveals no rhonchi or wheezes. Her skin has several "target" lesions scattered on her trunk and upper arms. A chest x-ray reveals a fine interstitial pattern with normal cardiac silhouette. She most likely is infected with what organism?

A. *Streptococcus pneumoniae*

B. *Chlamydia pneumoniae*

C. *Mycoplasma pneumoniae*

D. *Haemophilus influenzae*

E. Influenza A

QUESTION 48

A 12-month-old girl presents to your office for a well-child examination. She has been growing and developing well. She is taking solids well and has not had any gastrointestinal problems. She is happy and playful, and there are no abnormalities on physical examination. Routine screening reveals a lead level of 50 μg/dl. The child lives in a home built in 1980, and there is no peeling paint. The most appropriate initial management is:

A. Repeat lead level at 15 months of age.

B. Remove child from home; no other management needed.

C. If the home is proven to be lead free, no further evaluation or management needed.

D. Report this case. Search for source of lead. Initiate oral chelation therapy (succimer).

E. Hospitalize immediately for intravenous chelation therapy.

QUESTION 49

Which of the following is TRUE of neonates exposed to intrauterine maternal cocaine use?

A. They are frequently large for gestational age (LGA).

B. Their risk for sudden infant death syndrome (SIDS) is equal to that of infants not exposed to intrauterine drugs.

C. They are at increased risk of early onset necrotizing enterocolitis (NEC).

D. They are seldom premature.

E. Cocaine addicted neonates have normal sleep patterns.

QUESTION 50

A 6-year-old boy comes to your office for evaluation. He is not doing well in school and has a difficult time finishing his schoolwork in the time allotted. His mother tells you that his teacher is constantly having to redirect him, and that at times he is staring off into space daydreaming. When you question Mom, she has also noticed that he has recurrent episodes of brief staring spells. You examine the patient and order an EEG. What is the EEG likely to show?

A. Generalized symmetric 3-per-second spike and wave pattern

B. Generalized, diffuse slowing

C. Hypsarrhythmia

D. Localized spike and wave pattern

BLOCK TWO

QUESTIONS

QUESTION 51

A 16-year-old female presents to the emergency room with a fever of 102°F for 1 day, lower abdominal pain, and vaginal discharge. She admits to having unprotected sexual inter-course with a new male partner in the last 2 weeks. Her last menses was 1 week ago. She denies dysuria but complains of dyspareunia. Physical exam reveals bilateral lower abdominal tenderness, but no peritoneal signs. There is no suprapubic or costovertebral angle tenderness. On bimanual exam, she has right-sided adnexal tenderness, an erythematous, friable cervix with thick yellow discharge, and cervical motion ten-derness. Her cervix is normal in size. A serum HCG is negative, urinalysis is unremarkable and a cervical swab gram stain reveals gram-negative diplococci. Which of the following is the most likely diagnosis?

A. Pyelonephritis

B. Appendicitis

C. Ectopic pregnancy

D. Endometriosis

E. Pelvic inflammatory disease (PID)

QUESTION 52

A 6-year-old boy is seen in the office for a well visit. During the exam, strabismus is noted. You are concerned that he may be at risk for ambly-opia. Of the following, which is a TRUE state-ment concerning amblyopia?

A. Strabismus is the most common cause of amblyopia.

B. Amblyopia may result from watching too much TV.

C. Amblyopia is successfully treated at any age.

D. Treatment of amblyopia includes occlusion of the "bad" eye.

E. There are no clear risk factors for amblyopia.

QUESTION 53

While doing a preceptorship in a pediatrician's office, you perform a 2-week follow-up exam on a large newborn. You feel a firm small mass at the junction of the middle and distal thirds of the clavicle. Crepitus is also palpable. The child appears uncomfortable when lying on the affected side. The Moro reflex is diminished on the same side. These findings were present at birth also, but seem to be improving. The pedia-trician made a diagnosis of clavicular fracture. Which of the following statements is most likely true?

A. Clavicular fractures are almost never seen with modern day OB techniques.

B. These fractures are commonly associated with brachial nerve plexus injury or pneumothorax.

C. Clavicle fractures heal rapidly (in as little as 7–10 days).

D. Clavicular fractures are commonly associ-ated with shoulder dystocia.

E. This baby needs to be seen immediately by an orthopedist to ensure proper alignment.

QUESTION 54

A 12-year-old male presents to your office with a history of reactive airway disease since he was 6 years old. He wheezes throughout the day and requires a short and long-acting beta2-agonist daily. At night he complains of waking up frequently with cough and wheezing. He is currently taking a high-dose-inhaled steroid, a leukotriene inhibitor, and has just completed a 2-week oral steroid burst. His last peak expiratory flow (PEF) was <60% of predicted. How would you classify his asthma?

A.   Mild intermittent

B.   Mild persistent

C.   Moderate persistent

D.   Severe persistent

QUESTION 55

At the 6-month well-child visit, you notice that the baby's right eye is tearing excessively. On further questioning, the mom states that this has been happening since birth. On exam, the baby is thriving and the eye exam is otherwise normal. The most common cause of this condition is:

A.   Dacryocystitis

B.   Open globe

C.   Obstruction of the nasolacrimal duct

D.   Congenital glaucoma

E.   Chronic irritation from allergies

QUESTION 56

A 13-year-old boy comes into your office for a pre-participation sports physical. He has a harsh systolic ejection murmur at the right upper sternal border, which diminishes with the Valsalva maneuver. The murmur is preceded by an ejection click. The patient reports no symptoms at rest or with activity. Which advice is most appropriate for this patient?

A.   He should avoid all sports until he is evaluated further.

B.   He has an innocent flow murmur and is able to participate in all sports without restrictions.

C.   He has a pathologic murmur, but because he is asymptomatic, there is no reason to limit his participation in sports.

D.   There is no need for antibiotic prophylaxis prior to dental procedures.

QUESTION 57

A 7-year-old was admitted to PICU for altered mental status and suspected meningitis. During your exam, the patient developed a generalized tonic-clonic seizure. You promptly administer benzodiazepines, fluids, and ceftriaxone and vancomycin. Despite anticonvulsants, the seizure persists. Which complication of meningitis is most likely to cause a seizure that is refractory to the above treatments?

A.   Brain abscess

B.   Subdural empyema

C.   Hyponatremia from SIADH

D.   Elevated intracranial pressure (ICP)

E.   Complex febrile seizure

QUESTION 58

A 2-year-old presents to the office with an intermittent fever of 104°F for the past three days. The physical examination reveals no source of infection. The infant does not appear toxic, and the parents feel that he appears well between fevers. The differential diagnosis includes:

A. Rubella

B. Erythema infectiosum (Fifth disease)

C. Erythema toxicum

D. Roseola infantum

E. Meningitis

QUESTION 59

During a routine well-child visit, a patient's mother tells you she is concerned about her daughter's development. On further questioning you discover that the child knows six words, including "mama," walks alone, and recently started walking backwards. After you demonstrate, she is able to build a tower of two blocks and scribble with a pen, but cannot form a circle or a cross. You reassure the mother that her child is showing normal development for a child of:

A. 9 months

B. 12 months

C. 15 months

D. 24 months

E. 36 months

QUESTION 60

Which of the following is NOT a cause of proportionate short stature?

A. Malnutrition

B. Rickets

C. Teratogen exposure in utero

D. Turner's syndrome

E. Constitutional growth delay

QUESTION 61

A 2-year-old child presents to the clinic with a 1-month history of worsening anorexia, lower extremity edema, periorbital edema, and weight gain. You suspect nephrotic syndrome. All of the following help confirm your diagnosis EXCEPT:

A. Proteinuria

B. Hypoalbuminemia

C. Edema

D. Hypertriglyceridemia

E. Red blood cell casts

QUESTION 62

A 1-month-old female is brought to your office for her 1-month visit. Her mom states that she spits up about one tablespoon of milk-like material after each feed. It does not come up forcefully and contains no blood or bile. She takes 2 oz of Enfamil with iron every 2–3 hours. The spitting up often occurs after she is placed on her back in the crib. She is at the 25%ile for length, 5%ile for weight, and 25–50%ile for head circumference. On physical exam, the baby is well-hydrated with active bowel sounds and no palpable abdominal masses. The most likely diagnosis is:

A. Pyloric stenosis

B. Volvulus

C. Gastroesophageal reflux

D. Gastroenteritis

E. Tracheoesophageal fistula

QUESTION 63

A 14-month-old baby is brought to your office because of fatigue, irritability, and poor appetite. The child had been breast fed until 7 months of age, then switched to whole milk. The child drinks approximately 48 oz of milk daily, but eats little solid food yet. On physical examination, the child is found to have generalized pallor but no cardiorespiratory symptoms. The hemoglobin is 6 g/dl. Your initial approach is:

A. Order a complete blood count and reevaluate in 2 weeks.

B. Order a complete blood count and a serum lead level; check the child's home for lead.

C. Order a complete blood count and serum ferritin; initiate oral iron therapy and arrange to repeat the blood count in 2–4 weeks.

D. Admit the child to the hospital for a transfusion of packed red blood cells (20 ml/kg). Transfuse again until the hemoglobin is over 9 g/dl.

E. No laboratory tests or medicine are needed at this time. Add meats to the child's diet.

QUESTION 64

All of the following are appropriate steps in managing the patient in Figs. 64A and 64B EXCEPT:

A. Echocardiogram

B. Renal ultrasound

C. Chromosome analysis

D. Brain MRI

E. Growth hormone therapy

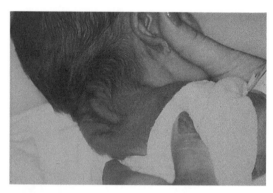

FIGURE 64A

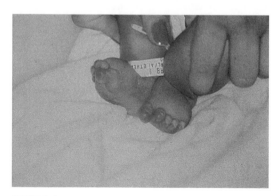

FIGURE 64B

QUESTION 65

A 12-month-old toddler presents with a 10-day history of acute otitis media unresponsive to amoxicillin therapy (80 mg/kg/day). On physical exam, he is febrile to 100.8°F. There is erythema and edema above the right ear with down and outward displacement of the pinna. The tympanic membrane is dull, opaque, and bulging. The light reflex is absent, and you are unable to move the tympanic membrane with insufflation. You are concerned that this patient has mastoiditis. If you are correct, what CT scan findings would verify your clinical diagnosis?

A. Normal ossicles and temporal bone, with soft tissue swelling behind the right ear

B. Destruction of septa between the mastoid cells on the right, with soft tissue swelling behind the right ear

C. Free fluid surrounding the ossicles with normal temporal bone and clear mastoid cells on the right

D. Normal CT scan

QUESTION 66

An 18-month-old boy is brought to the emergency room by his parents. He has been wheezing since this morning. He had a runny nose and fever 2 days prior to this visit, which have resolved. There is no family history of asthma. On exam, the child appears active and in no acute distress. You notice nasal flaring and there is wheezing in the right lung fields. A chest x-ray reveals hyperinflation of the right lung and there is no infiltrate. The most appropriate next step in management is:

A. Reassurance and home treatment with a beta agonist via small volume nebulizer

B. Initiate oral prednisone treatment for a 5-day course

C. Immediate chest tube placement

D. Bronchoscopy

E. Treatment with racemic epinephrine via small volume nebulizer

QUESTION 67

Which of the following is NOT true of congenital cytomegalovirus (CMV) infection?

A. With acute fulminant infection, CMV may present with hepatosplenomegaly, petechiae, jaundice, intrauterine growth retardation, thrombocytopenia, and elevated direct hyperbilirubinemia.

B. Periventricular calcifications may be present.

C. Children may develop mental retardation.

D. There is no evidence of hearing loss.

E. Microcephaly may be present at birth.

QUESTION 68

An 8-year-old boy is brought to your office by his mother for evaluation. She is concerned about his poor school performance. He is much "slower" to learn than the other children in his school. She has noted several hyperpigmented macular lesions on his forehead, and his "acne" seems to be getting worse. You note that he has two flat, hypopigmented macules on his trunk. You are concerned that he may have the clinical manifestations of:

A. Sturge–Weber syndrome

B. Von Hippel–Lindau disease

C. Neurofibromatosis

D. Tuberous sclerosis

FIGURE 68A

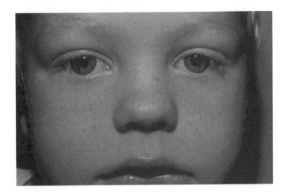

FIGURE 68B

QUESTION 69

Which of the following is NOT a major manifestation in the Jones criteria for diagnosis of rheumatic fever?

A. Fever

B. Chorea

C. Carditis

D. Erythema marginatum

E. Subcutaneous nodules

QUESTION 70

All of the following groups are at high risk for eye pathology and will require ophthalmologic follow-up EXCEPT:

A. Children with a family history of amblyopia

B. Premature infants

C. Patients with cerebral palsy

D. Patients exposed to TORCH infections in utero

E. Patients with frequent conjunctivitis

QUESTION 71

You are called to the newborn nursery to see a baby with a deformed foot. The affected foot is shorter and smaller than the other. The heel is turned downward and inward, while the front of the foot is curved inwardly. The medial crease of the foot is accentuated. The foot has almost no flexibility. You diagnose a unilateral rigid clubfoot deformity. Which statement is NOT true?

A. Rigid clubfoot may require surgery.

B. Some of these children have other deformities, i.e., spina bifida, neuromuscular deformity.

C. This deformity usually prevents a child from standing and walking.

D. After surgery, long-term observation and bracing is usually necessary.

E. These children are active and participate with peers in the usual physical activities.

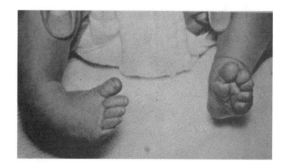

FIGURE 71

QUESTION 72

Cystic fibrosis may present in the neonatal period or in adults. Which of the following are possible complications associated with cystic fibrosis?

A. Rectal prolapse

B. Protein-calorie malnutrition

C. Nasal polyps

D. Male infertility

E. All of the above

QUESTION 73

You live in Arizona where many families have home swimming pools and the drowning rates are high. The mother of a 5-month-old child asks you about the best ways to prevent drowning. Which one of the following items will be included in the advice you will give her?

A. In order to prevent drowning, the American Academy of Pediatrics recommends swimming lessons starting at age 6 months.

B. Most children struggle and make loud noises when they fall into a pool, so parents should always listen carefully.

C. Pool fencing has not been shown to prevent drowning and is a waste of money.

D. Toys and tricycles should be kept away from the pool area, so they will not attract children to the pool.

E. Special supporting rings are a good method to prevent bathtub drowning.

QUESTION 74

You are called to evaluate a term newborn in the delivery room. The pregnancy and delivery were uneventful, but the baby has remained cyanotic despite routine delivery room care. A hyperoxia test is performed; the results of which are printed below:

$$FiO_2 = 0.21 \qquad FiO_2 = 1.00$$
$$PaO_2 = 30 \qquad PaO_2 = 40$$

Which statement is the correct interpretation of the test results above?

A. The test results suggest that the baby has a cardiac defect involving restricted pulmonary blood flow or a separate circulation.

B. The baby has a normal PaO_2 for a newborn.

C. The test results suggest that the baby has underlying neurologic disease.

D. The test results suggest that the baby has a cardiac defect involving complete mixing without restricted pulmonary blood flow.

QUESTION 75

The infant in the picture below presented to the pediatric intensive care unit with T39°C, decreased urine output, P190, BP 60/30, disseminated intravascular coagulation (DIC), and a palpable rash. Immediate steps should include all of the following EXCEPT:

A. Antibiotic treatment to cover gram-positive cocci, meningococci, and gram-negative bacilli

B. Topical antibiotics applied to all blisters noted on physical exam after they have been appropriately drained and unroofed

C. Isolation of the hospitalized patient

D. Initial intravascular support with normal saline and/or lactated-ringers

E. Blood culture (preferably before antibiotics)

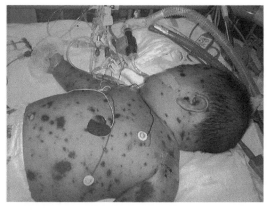

FIGURE 75

QUESTION 76

A 3-week-old Caucasian male is brought to your clinic by his parents for a red growth on his face. He was a healthy term baby weighing 3650 g. He was seen previously in your office at 3 days of age and had no skin findings at that time. There is a $1\frac{1}{2}$ cm × 2 cm bright red, raised lesion on the left temple. It is soft and nontender to palpation without blanching. The parents are very concerned. You advise them:

A. The lesion is highly concerning and a punch biopsy should be performed immediately.

B. This lesion is consistent with a benign condition and will disappear before 1 year of age.

C. The lesion is consistent with a benign condition that will likely increase in size over the first year, then begin to fade and disappear entirely by school age without treatment.

D. The lesion should be injected with steroids to produce the best cosmetic result.

E. This is an infectious lesion and should be treated with high dose IV antibiotics.

QUESTION 77

An 18-month-old boy presents for a well-child visit. Upon entering the room, you notice him playing with toys, touching everything in the room, and speaking to his mother in 2-word phrases. According to Piaget's stages of cognitive development, he would best be classified in:

A. Sensorimotor stage

B. Preoperational stage

C. Concrete operational stage

D. Abstract operational stage

E. Formal operational stage

QUESTION 78

A 10-year-old boy comes to the office for evaluation of short stature. His height and weight are below the 5th percentile for his age, but his growth velocity is normal. The child has otherwise been healthy. Physical exam reveals an immature male with no evidence of pubertal development and his bone age is that of a 6-year-old male. What is the most likely diagnosis?

A. Constitutional growth delay

B. Familial short stature

C. Primary hypothyroidism

D. Growth hormone deficiency

E. Chronic systemic disease

QUESTION 79

A 1-year-old child presents to the emergency room with a 3-day history of dehydration. Physical examination of the infant is consistent with 10% dehydration. Serum sodium level is 165. All of the following about hypernatremic dehydration are true EXCEPT:

A. Subdural hematomas may occur as a result of hypernatremia.

B. Hypernatremia may be caused when improperly mixed formulas are used.

C. Normal saline boluses should be given until the infant is stable.

D. Fluid should be given to rapidly reduce the serum Na in less than 24 hours.

E. Hypernatremia is seen in about 10–15% of patients with diarrhea.

QUESTION 80

A 15-month-old male is brought to the pediatrician's office because he seems much smaller than his two older brothers were at that age. His mother states that he has been generally healthy except for two episodes of otitis media and an occasional "cold." He began walking at $11\frac{1}{2}$ months and can now say "mama," "dada," "byebye," and the names of his brothers and dog. What is the most appropriate first step in evaluating his size?

A. Perform a Denver Developmental Screening Test.

B. Ask Mom to complete a 3-day food diary.

C. Send blood for quantitative immunoglobulins.

D. Plot his height and weight on the growth chart and compare to previous charts.

E. Obtain a sweat chloride test.

QUESTION 81

A 12-year-old boy comes to your office because of unexplained bruising. There is no history of previous bruising or excessive bleeding. The child has had no fever or respiratory symptoms. Three weeks ago, the child had chickenpox (varicella). On examination today, the patient is cooperative and in no acute distress. A complete CBC has the following results: hemoglobin is 12 g/dl, WBC is 12,500, and the platelet count is 45,000. Large platelets are seen on the smear. Prothrombin time and activated partial thromboplastin time (APPT) are normal. Treatment of this child should include:

A. Platelet transfusion

B. Oral prednisone

C. Admit the child to the intensive care unit to observe for intracranial bleeding.

D. Reassure the parents that no specific treatment is needed at this time.

E. Administer intravenous immunoglobulin (IVIG).

QUESTION 82

A 2-year-old boy presents to your office for evaluation of speech delay. On examination, he is at the 90th percentile for height, 50th percentile for weight, and greater than the 98th percentile for head circumference. He has a long face with large protuberant ears, velvety skin, and is extremely hyperactive with no eye contact. Which of the following is true?

A. Both parents are gene carriers for this condition.

B. He has small genitalia and undescended testicles.

C. His mother is a gene carrier for this condition.

D. The parents have a 50% recurrence risk for any future pregnancy.

E. Chromosome analysis will reveal an extra chromosome.

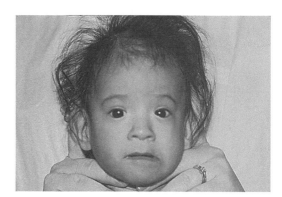

FIGURE 82

QUESTION 83

Which of the following is NOT true regarding the use of Palivizumab in the prevention of respiratory synctial virus (RSV) infection?

A. Palivizumab is a monoclonal antibody.

B. It should be given every other month for six doses for infants/children that meet specific criteria.

C. A 6-month-old term infant with a ventricular septal defect should receive Palivizumab at the beginning of RSV season.

D. A 4-month-old ex-28 weeks gestation female should receive Palivizumab at the beginning of RSV season.

E. A 3-month-old ex-31 weeks gestation male with bronchopulmonary dysplasia (BPD) on 0.1 L O_2 continuously should receive Palivizumab at the beginning of RSV season.

QUESTION 84

You are working in the emergency department of a large urban hospital when a 4-month-old boy is brought in with a soft swelling on the right side of the head. The boy's mother says that the baby has been eating and acting normally. She is unaware of any head trauma. The baby appears happy and playful, and there are no old bruises or scars. A CT scan of the head reveals no intracranial hemorrhage, but a linear skull fracture of the right parietal bone is seen by the radiologist. What would you do next?

A. Tell the mother you are going to call the police and have her arrested for child abuse.

B. Explain to the mother that linear skull fractures are dangerous and are often associated with permanent brain damage.

C. Admit the child to the pediatric intensive care unit for careful monitoring of neurological and respiratory status.

D. Start a workup for suspected non-accidental trauma, including radiographic studies to look for new and old fractures.

E. Report the case to Child Protective Services, then discharge the baby to home.

QUESTION 85

An intraventricular hemorrhage with ventricular dilatation is considered what grade based on the Papile Grading System in neonates?

A. Grade 1

B. Grade 2

C. Grade 3

D. Grade 4

E. None of the above

QUESTION 86

An 11-year-old boy with an underlying seizure disorder presents to the emergency department in status epilepticus. Which of the following interventions would NOT be indicated urgently?

A. Administration of rectal diazepam

B. Urgent CT scan of the head

C. IV administration of lorazepam

D. IV loading dose of phenytoin

E. Correction of any abnormalities of the airway, breathing, and circulation

QUESTION 87

A 26-month-old child presents for follow-up of suspected iron deficiency anemia. Routine screening 8 weeks ago revealed a hypochromic, microcytic anemia (hemoglobin 9.0 g/dl and MCV 65 fl). The patient was empirically started on oral iron at that time. The child eats a well-balanced diet and drinks about 10 oz of milk daily from a cup. The patient's family is originally from the Middle East and a brother also has mild anemia with microcytosis. The child has never missed a well-child checkup and is completely immunized. On physical examination, the child appears normal aside from pale conjunctiva. A repeat blood count is unchanged from the previous values. The next appropriate step in management is:

A. Advise the patient to drink less milk and eat more iron containing foods.

B. Order a hemoglobin electrophoresis to evaluate for thalassemia.

C. Reassure the parents that anemia from poor eating is common in 2-year-olds.

D. Order a transfusion of packed red blood cells.

E. Order an injection of iron and report the family to Child Protective Services.

QUESTION 88

A red eye in an infant less than 2 weeks of age may be explained by all of the following EXCEPT:

A. *Chlamydia trachomatis* or *Neisseria gonorrhoeae*

B. Herpes simplex virus

C. Chemical irritation after silver nitrate prophylaxis

D. Excessive tearing from a blocked naso-lacrimal duct

E. *Staphylococcus aureus*

QUESTION 89

You are called to the emergency room to see a 7-year-old with an injured arm after a fall. The child holds the arm in flexion and braces it with the other arm. There is remarkable point tenderness in the distal radius. You obtain an x-ray which shows a buckle fracture. Which statement is false?

A. Forearm fractures are the most common location for children's fractures.

B. Special attention should be given to any rotation or angulation problems with these fractures.

C. Forearm fractures are usually sustained by a fall on an outstretched hand.

D. Buckle fractures have a high incidence of non-union.

E. Forearm fractures may be buckle fractures (compression), greenstick (incomplete), or complete.

QUESTION 90

Which of the following would NOT be seen in patients with pulmonary hemosiderosis?

A. Frothy, blood tinged sputum

B. A normal chest x-ray

C. Association with a milk allergy

D. Alveolar hemorrhages on lung biopsy

E. Iron deficiency anemia

QUESTION 91

A 2-year-old girl with well-demarcated bilateral "stocking" distribution scald burns is brought to your office by her mother. The mother says that the child climbed into the bathtub before the mother had a chance to test the water temperature. Which of the following items makes you highly suspicious that this injury is due to non-accidental trauma?

A. The mother brought the patient to your office immediately, without applying any ointment or dressing.

B. The bilateral sharply demarcated "stocking" distribution of the burns.

C. The type of burn (scald).

D. The presence of satellite burns caused by splashing water.

E. The parents had not turned the temperature settings on the hot water heater down to a safe level.

QUESTION 92

An infant admitted with sepsis has a gram stain of the blood that shows intracellular and extracellular gram-negative diplocci, which of the following would be an appropriate next step?

A. Ceftriaxone for the pregnant third-year resident who intubated the patient on arrival to the intensive care unit

B. Fourteen doses of rifampin (every 12 hours) given to all close contacts (household, daycare) and all hospital contacts with respiratory secretion contact

C. High-resolution chromosomal studies if this represented recurrent disease

D. Vaccination for a sibling with a past medical history significant for multiple treatments for otitis media

E. Continued respiratory isolation for the full course of antibiotics (7 days)

QUESTION 93

You are seeing a previously healthy, 8-month-old male with a 2- to 3-week history of a rash. The rash started on the cheeks and has subsequently spread to involve the trunk and extremities. He is bathed once daily and his mother has not been using ointments or creams. She does not use detergent when washing his clothes. He has not had any recent URI symptoms or fever. Family history is significant only for seasonal allergies in the maternal great-grandmother. Physical examination shows a well-nourished male, who is afebrile and playful. Examination of the skin reveals lesions on the extensor surfaces of the upper and lower extremities which are red and dry with small papules, mild scaling, and areas of excoriation. Compared with the general population, his risk for developing asthma is which of the following?

A. Greater than the general population

B. Less than the general population

C. Equal to that of the general population

D. There is no clear association

QUESTION 94

In males, the initiation sequence of sexual development is:

A. Pubic hair, height growth spurt, penile enlargement, testicular enlargement

B. Penile enlargement, testicular enlargement, height growth spurt, pubic hair

C. Pubic hair, testicular enlargement, penile enlargement, height growth spurt

D. Testicular enlargement, penile enlargement, height growth spurt, pubic hair

QUESTION 95

A 6-month-old infant presents to clinic with a 1-day history of diarrhea. No emesis has occurred. The infant appears about 3–5% dehydrated. The initial management should include which of the following?

A. Oral rehydration with observation in the clinic

B. Perform intraosseous access for rehydration.

C. Perform a lumbar puncture followed by antibiotic therapy.

D. Recommend that the mother give fruit juice until the diarrhea resolves.

E. Hospital admission

QUESTION 96

You are seeing a previously healthy 4-year-old girl with a 4-day history of fever, itching truncal rash, and bilateral foot pain. Her fever has been as high as 103°F. The rash is decribed by her mother as "feeling rough." She complains of pain in her feet when she is wearing shoes, and has refused to walk today. She has not had any recent URI symptoms and there has been no emesis or diarrhea. There have been no known ill contacts; however, she is in daycare. Physical examination is significant for a mildly dehydrated female who appears ill, but not toxic. Her temperature is 38.5°C. There is bilateral bulbar and conjunctival injection without exudate. Her lips are dry and cracked. Her tongue is erythematous and without lesions. There are no palatal petechia and her posterior pharynx is benign without exudate. She has tender anterior cervical lymph nodes measuring 2–3 cm. Lungs are clear. There are no murmurs, and extremities are well perfused. Examination of the skin reveals a fine mildly erythematous sandpaper-like truncal rash with areas of excoriation. Both hands and feet are edematous. A rapid strep test is negative. The most appropriate next step would be:

A. Obtain a CBC, blood culture, and give an IM dose of a broad spectrum antibiotic with plans to reexamine her in the morning.

B. Send a throat swab for culture and hold antibiotics pending results.

C. Treat her empirically for strep throat and await the culture results.

D. Admit her, obtain basic laboratory studies including a CXR and consult a pediatric cardiologist.

E. Admit her for rehydration therapy and observation.

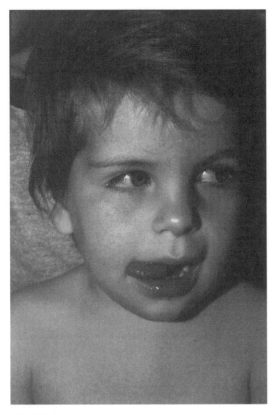

FIGURE 96A

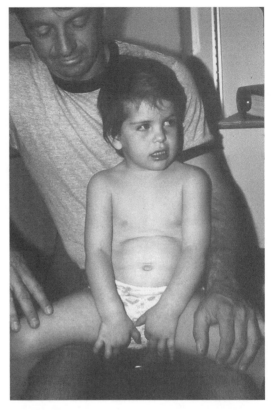

FIGURE 96B

FIGURE 96C

QUESTION 97

A parent comes to your office for a well-child visit. You notice the patient hopping to the exam room, singing "London Bridge Is Falling Down." Mom states the patient does a great job playing cooperatively. The age of the patient according to his observed milestones may best be described as:

A. 2 years old

B. 3 years old

C. 4 years old

D. 5 years old

E. 6 years old

QUESTION 98

A 4-year-old female presents with ulcers on her tongue and oral mucosa. The patient refuses to eat due to pain in her mouth. Her temperature is 38.3°C (101°F). A maculopapular, vesicular rash is also noted on the hands, feet, and buttocks. The patient is diagnosed with hand-foot-and-mouth disease. This common disease of children is caused by:

A. Paramyxovirus

B. Rubella virus

C. Herpes virus 6

D. Parvovirus B-19

E. Coxsackie A viruses

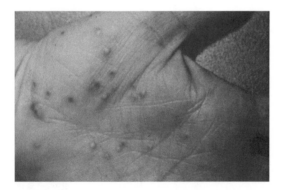

FIGURE 98A

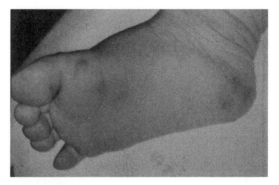

FIGURE 98B

QUESTION 99

A toddler presents to your office with his arm in flexion and his hand in pronation. He will not let anyone touch that arm. There is no history of trauma. The attending physician performs a rapid maneuver, and within 20 minutes the child is using the arm normally. Which of the following is true?

A. X-rays are always in order.

B. This is almost pathognomonic of child abuse.

C. This problem requires casting.

D. This almost certainly is subluxation of the radial head.

QUESTION 100

A 4-month-old infant presents with a 5-day history of vomiting and diarrhea. Subsequently, she develops tonic/clonic seizures unresponsive to antiepileptic medication. A possible cause of seizures in this patient may be due to:

A. Zinc deficiency

B. Celiac disease

C. Hyperchloremia

D. Hyponatremia

E. Hyperglycemia

BLOCK **ONE**

ANSWERS

ANSWER 1

C. Truncus arteriosus is a rare form of congenital heart disease which presents with moderate cyanosis at birth due to the fact that there is complete mixing of systemic and pulmonary venous blood.

A. Although tetralogy of Fallot is usually also associated with cyanosis, there must be at least 5 g/dl of deoxygenated hemoglobin present in order for cyanosis to be present. Therefore, in severely anemic states, cyanosis may not be present.

B. Coarctation is not typically a cyanotic lesion. Femoral pulses will be weak or absent with upper extremity hypertension.

D. VSD is the most common congenital heart disease. A severe lesion may result in congestive heart failure but without cyanosis.

E. ASD is not a cyanotic lesion, although high flow or secundum lesions may require SBE prophylaxis.

ANSWER 2

C. Anaphylactic shock from latex allergy has been associated with myelomeningocele patients. Some authors suggest this may be the result of chronic exposure to latex (i.e., during repeated urinary catheterizations). The timing as well as symptoms (wheezing) suggest anaphylaxis.

A. to E. Shock, regardless of the etiology, will have similar clinical manifestations (i.e., hypotension and usually tachycardia). Signs of sepsis may include fever or rash or evidence of focal infection, cardiogenic shock may be associated with hepatomegaly, gallop rhythm, or cyanosis, and a clue to hypovolemic shock may come from a history of vomiting, diarrhea, or poor intake. The respiratory symptoms and wheezing should lead to consideration of latex allergy in this case.

ANSWER 3

C. This rash is bullous impetigo caused by *Staphylococcus aureus*. It is effectively treated with a topical antibiotic which includes coverage for *Staphylococcus*.

A. Neosporin may be sensitizing due to the neomycin component.

B. The rash is not candidal and steroids are not indicated.

D. Desitin is indicated for contact (irritant) diaper dermatitis and its prevention.

E. Amoxicillin does not have good staphylococcal coverage and systemic treatment is probably not necessary.

ANSWER 4

C. Bone age is not a developmental milestone, but rather a physiologic standard of growth based on radiographs.

All of the remaining choices are recognized developmental milestones.

ANSWER 5

B. The serum blood glucose is grossly elevated in diabetic ketoacidois (DKA) because the absence of insulin in the bloodstream makes glucose unable to enter the cells.

A. Although not specific for DKA, hyperpnea is indicative of the acidosis associated with DKA.

C. Polyuria, polydipsia, and fatigue are the result of the osmotic diuresis seen with hyperglycemia.

D. Ketoacidosis is a hallmark of DKA.

E. Ketones are seen in the urine during DKA, or any other catabolic state where proteins are being used as a major energy source.

ANSWER 6

B. This is the classic presentation of pyloric stenosis. It presents most commonly in a 6-week to 3-month-old first-born male infant. Hypochloremic, hypokalemic metabolic acidosis is seen secondary to the loss of HCl and a compensatory H^+/K^+ exchange in the kidneys.

A. Gastroesophageal reflux disease is common, although it generally does not cause dehydration.

C. In the setting of a viral infection, the infant would likely have fever and diarrhea.

D. Duodenal atresia presents with vomiting (usually bilious) in the first few days of life.

E. Hirschsprung's disease is characterized by constipation.

ANSWER 7

C. Shigella gastroenteritis is characterized by blood in the stools, high fever, watery diarrhea, a high stool volume, elevated white blood cell count, and bandemia.

A. Intussusception occurs more commonly in younger patients.

B. Acute onset of severe, bloody diarrhea is not typical of viral gastroenteritis.

D. Ulcerative colitis is uncommon in this age group and may have a more chronic course.

E. Diarrhea and fever are not characteristic of Meckel's diverticulum, and abdominal pain is usually present.

ANSWER 8

B. Acute onset of jaundice and abnormal red cell morphology are typical of hemolytic anemia. Stressors such as infection or certain medications may trigger hemolysis. G6PD deficiency is transmitted as an X-linked recessive trait, so males are primarily affected. Children of Mediterranean and African-American background are at greatest risk.

A. Iron deficiency anemia is associated with a microcytic, not normocytic, anemia.

C. Sickle cell disease is most common in children of African-American descent. Sickle cells are seen on the peripheral blood smear.

D. Thalassemia trait is associated with microcytic anemia. The hemoglobin is usually between 9 and 10 g/dl.

E. The mean corpuscular volume is abnormally large in folate deficiency.

ANSWER 9

D. Although the spectrum of congenital anomalies seen in infants of diabetic mothers (IDM) is broad, abdominal wall defects are not typically seen. Diabetic embryopathy is the most common teratogenic disorder and occurs secondary to persistent hyperglycemia in maternal insulin dependent diabetes mellitus (IDDM). Congenital anomalies are seen in 10% of exposed infants, compared to 2–5% of the general population.

A. Sacral agenesis with lumbar vertebral anomalies, poor growth of the caudal region, distal spinal cord disruption, and other anomalies are common in IDM.

B. IDM infants are often large for gestational age with increased body size and visceromegaly.

C. Congenital heart disease is very common among IDM infants and includes transient hypertrophic subaortic stenosis, transposition of the great vessels, ASD, VSD, and aortic coarctation.

E. Other midline defects, including CNS anomalies such as anencephaly, myelomeningocele, hydrocephalus, and microcephaly, are also common in IDM.

ANSWER 10

A. Is incorrect and could lead to airway obstruction.

B. Children with epiglottitis should be allowed to sit and lean forward to help their airway open. All of these signs and symptoms are typical. As these children may obstruct totally at any time, rapid preparations must be made to maintain an airway.

C. Reassurance and allowing the mother to hold the child will decrease distress while you arrange proper treatment.

D. This child should be evaluated in a controlled setting, (i.e., in an operating room in the presence of an anesthesiologist and/or otolaryngologist) so that rapid airway control may be achieved if necessary.

E. Sudden pulmonary arrest is a likely occurrence in children with epiglottitis and should be anticipated.

ANSWER 11

D. The first priority in a comatose, unresponsive, vomiting patient is management of airway, bleeding, and circulation (ABC's). Establishment of a secure airway is the first and most important step.

A. Syrup of ipecac should not be used in comatose patients.

B. It will be important to learn what medicines have been ingested, but this is not the first priority.

C. Gastric lavage is not likely to be beneficial more than 60 minutes after an ingestion. In order to prevent pulmonary aspiration, gastric lavage should never be performed in a comatose patient prior to placing an endotracheal tube.

E. This child will require admission to an intensive care unit after stabilization.

ANSWER 12

A. The fifth and sixth cervical spinal nerves are affected.

B. Frequently seen with large, hypotonic infants that require increased traction on the head and neck during a vaginal delivery.

C. The grasp reflex is not affected and should be intact.

D. Because of the brachial plexus injury in C5 and C6 spinal nerves, the Moro, biceps, and radial reflexes are absent on the injured side.

E. Because of the brachial plexus injury in C5 and C6 spinal nerves, the neonate's arm would be adducted and internally rotated with the elbow extended, the forearm in pronation, and the wrist in flexion.

ANSWER 13

B. This patient most likely experienced a simple febrile seizure. Most febrile seizures last less than 10 minutes, are generalized and nonfocal, and do not recur within 24 hours. These simple febrile seizures do not require evaluation beyond determining and treating the source of the fever and educating parents.

A. There is no need for neuroimaging studies in a case of simple febrile seizure.

C. There is no need for an EEG in the case of a simple febrile seizure with a negative family history, normal neurologic exam, and normal development.

D. Although anticonvulsant medications are sometimes used for recurrent episodes of febrile seizures, the initial simple febrile seizure does not warrant treatment with anticonvulsant drugs.

E. A lumbar puncture is not indicated in this patient unless the physical exam revealed symptoms suggestive of meningitis or encephalitis. In this case, the examination is normal except for the otitis media, the source of the fever.

ANSWER 14

B. Increasing caloric density of feedings and careful frequent follow-up of weight gain is a good first step. If there is no improvement with good caloric intake, then consider hospitalization.

A. This is an expensive approach and usually unnecessary.

C. This child is too young to start solid foods and the caloric content of solid foods is lower.

D. This approach is too aggressive without more information and evidence of neglect.

E. Switching to another cow's milk based formula is no significant change and would not provide additional calories.

ANSWER 15

A. Retinal hemorrhages may indicate shaken baby syndrome and, in some cases, may be the only verifiable sign of child abuse.

B. Conjunctivitis is the result of an infection, allergy, or contact irritation and is not typical of abuse.

C. Strabismus is not a typical early finding in an abuse case.

D. May be seen as a late finding if an abused child has suffered severe trauma or retinal detachment, but would not coexist with new bruises.

E. Dacryocystitis results from infection of the lacrimal duct and is not associated with trauma.

ANSWER 16

C. Tegretol; all of the others are associated with acne.

ANSWER 17

C. Metabolic disturbances are frequent causes of apnea in preterm and term infants. However, hypoglycemia, NOT hyperglycemia, may present as apnea in the newborn.

A. Sepsis in a newborn may frequently present as new onset apnea or as an increase in apneic events in preterm infants. It may be the only symptom.

B. Apnea of prematurity is a diagnosis of exclusion in preterm infants <37 weeks gestation who present with apnea after birth. It is centrally mediated and metabolic, infectious, and structural anomalies need to be excluded.

D. Severe hypoxemia in utero or during delivery may result in central apnea, secondary to neurologic damage.

E. Intraventricular hemorrhage may cause apnea in preterm and term infants. It may be associated with a decreasing hematocrit. Head ultrasound will reveal the hemorrhage.

ANSWER 18

D. Enuresis is a common problem that is usually self-limited, but treatment with buzzer alarm conditioning devices has been shown to be effective in about 75% of cases.

A. Unless there is a history of urinary tract infection or an abnormal urinary stream, cultures and radiographic studies are not necessary.

B. Intervention, when enuresis persists beyond 7–8 years of age, may decrease stress and embarrassment.

C. While medications may work initially, most children start wetting again as soon as the medication is stopped. Since desmopressin is very expensive and imipramine may cause serious side effects if overdosed, medications should probably not be used as initial cultures and radiographic studies are not necessary.

E. Punishment and restriction of fluid have not been shown to be effective treatments for enuresis.

ANSWER 19

D. "Tet spells" are caused by an increase in right ventricular outflow resistance leading to an increase in right-to-left shunting of blood, resulting in worsening cyanosis. These spells may resolve spontaneously, but may require treatment if they are sustained. The treatment of the spells is to diminish right-to-left shunting by increasing systemic vascular resistance (with the administration of neo-synephrine or the knee-to-chest maneuver), or decreasing pulmonary vascular resistance (with the administration of morphine sulfate). Volume is usually given concomitantly to increase the systemic blood pressure, which will also minimize right-to-left shunting. The administration of nitroglycerin would be expected to worsen a "tet spell," as its vasodilator effects would lead to a decrease in systemic blood pressure and worsening right-to-left shunt.

ANSWER 20

D. Initial fluid resuscitation requires isotonic solution (NS/LR). Other solutions may result in further complications with electrolyte disturbances and inadequate treatment of shock. The estimation of deficit is important in small infants and children because of the relatively small intravascular volume, and over- or under-treatment can have serious consequences. Deficit is best calculated by loss of weight, but often pre-dehydration weights are unknown. Severe signs of dehydration, such as sunken fontanelle, lethargy, and dry mucous membranes place the deficit at 10% or greater. A 4-kg infant with 10% dehydration has a 400-cc deficit. An infant with slightly dry mucous membranes, tachycardia, and concentrated urine would suggest a dehydration of about 5%.

ANSWER 21

D. and E. The axillae and inguinal areas are not exposed to contact with irritants and are not typically dry areas. The axillae and groin are areas which are usually covered by clothing or diapers and are unlikely to come in contact with contact irritants. The head, scalp, face, and eyebrows are all oily areas due to an increased concentration of sebaceous glands and stimulation from maternal hormones.

A. Infantile acne is another name for seborrhea in infants.

B. Seborrhea is a common rash in infants. It occurs when sebaceous glands are stimulated by increased maternal hormones during pregnancy.

C. Cradle cap is another form of seborrhea.

ANSWER 22

B. Developmental delay refers to a performance significantly below average in a given skill area. This boy's language development is delayed to about the 21-month-old level.

A. The language development described is normal for a 21-month-old, not a 4-year-old.

C. Developmental quotient is defined as (developmental age divided by chronological age) × 100.

D. Refers to a substantial difference in the rate of development between two skill areas.

E. Refers to non-sequential development within a given area of skill.

ANSWER 23

C. The immediate goal in treating DKA is to restore intravascular volume, paying attention to electrolyte losses associated with DKA, especially potassium and phosphate. Intravenous administration of insulin follows to reverse the catabolic state and the ketosis.

A. The serum glucose is elevated in DKA and supplemental administration of dextrose is not helpful.

B. Sodium bicarbonate is usually not necessary to correct the acidosis and is certainly not the immediate treatment indicated.

D. Antibiotic administration should be initiated only if an infection has been identified.

E. Screening siblings is not indicated and is certainly not addressed as an immediate issue when a patient presents in DKA.

ANSWER 24

C. This is a classic presentation of insulin dependent diabetes mellitus. Management includes fluid resuscitation, administration of insulin, dietary adjustment, and patient and family education. Metabolic acidosis is seen in diabetes due to elevated ketones, not alkalosis.

A. Dehydration occurs due to osmotic dehydration and increased urination.

B. Kussmaul respirations describe hyperpnea secondary to metabolic acidosis.

D. Hyperglycemia occurs secondary to insulin resistance and pancreatic insufficiency.

E. Glucosuria occurs when the serum glucose is elevated above a threshold level, stimulating glucose losses in the urine.

ANSWER 25

D. This child most likely has a viral gastroenteritis as there is no blood, no fever, the diarrhea is not severe, and the illness is acute. It is best to manage this patient with dietary changes to rest the gastrointestinal tract and provide hydration. If there is no improvement in 2–3 days, consider further workup.

A. Stool culture and sensitivity are not cost effective until the illness is prolonged >7–14 days or unless there is a history of bloody stools.

B. Parasitic causes are less likely in patients this young without a history of foreign travel.

C. Oral antidiarrheal medications are not necessary, and the risk of obstruction is greater than the benefits.

E. Antibiotics are not necessary because this illness is viral, and antibiotics may worsen the symptoms.

ANSWER 26

1.E. Babies are born with relatively high hemoglobin levels. These levels fall to a nadir at about 2 months of life. No treatment is needed.

2.D. Microcytic anemia with a high RDW is typical of iron deficiency. Children who drink large amounts of whole milk are at risk for development of this type of anemia due to microscopic blood loss in stool.

3.C. About 2–3% of the African-American population have heterozygous alpha thalassemia (alpha thalassemia trait). These children have a large number of very small red blood cells. They may have very mild anemia. The RDW, which is high in iron deficiency, is normal in alpha thalassemia trait.

4.A. Goat's milk feeding may result in folic acid deficiency and macrocytic anemia.

5.B. Children with sickle cell anemia have rapid breakdown of red cells. The bone marrow is very active, causing an elevated reticulocyte count, typical of all types of hemolytic anemias.

ANSWER 27

D. Dietary restriction for affected females with PKU must be lifelong, due to the teratogenic potential of maternal PKU, which may cause microcephaly, mental retardation, congenital heart defects, and other anomalies in the fetus.

A. This is true, as PKU is an autosomal recessive condition.

B. Strict dietary management with monitoring of phenylalanine blood levels is essential.

C. Patients who are treated from birth and closely monitored have a good prognosis for normal intellectual development.

E. Patients whose treatment is delayed or not closely monitored will become mentally retarded.

ANSWER 28

E. Varicella has an incubation period of 11–21 days.

A. The child should be placed in respiratory isolation until there are no new lesions and all of the lesions are scabbed.

B. Varicella is very dangerous in immunocompromised hosts and should be treated aggressively in those cases.

C. Once all lesions are crusted, varicella is no longer contagious.

D. The pruritus with varicella may result in scratching, scarring, and secondary infection.

ANSWER 29

C. Since 1992, when the American Academy of Pediatrics recommended babies be put to sleep on their backs, there has been a dramatic decrease in the incidence of SIDS.

A. Apnea monitors are usually used after a severe life-threatening event or when a baby is having apneic episodes or periodic breathing. Some experts believe in using an apnea monitor for siblings of a SIDS victim. In this child's case, there is no reason to use a home apnea monitor.

B. Only babies with certain problems, such as severe gastroesophageal reflux or craniofacial abnormalities, should be placed to sleep in a prone position.

D. A sleep study is not indicated for this asymptomatic baby with no family history of apnea.

E. It is important to pay attention to the mother's concerns. In this case, placing the baby to sleep on her back will reduce the risk of SIDS significantly.

ANSWER 30

E. Absence of blood in the diarrheal stools should point you away from the diagnosis of NEC. Trace guaiac positivity to grossly bloody stools may be present with NEC.

A. A fixed position loop of bowel, ileus, on abdominal films is consistent with NEC. Pneumatosis cystoides intestinalis is the radiologic hallmark. Thickened bowel wall, gross perforation with free air, and hepatic venous air may also be seen.

B. Temperature instability is a non-specific sign in neonates but is frequently seen with NEC. It may also be seen with prematurity alone or with sepsis.

C. Increased gastric aspirates are seen secondary to the development of an ileus. When NEC is suspected, feeds should be discontinued immediately.

D. Oliguria may be seen in the presence of hypotension and decreased renal perfusion.

ANSWER 31

D. Alpha-fetoprotein is an excellent screening tool used during pregnancy to identify a fetus with a suspected neural tube defect if measured between 16–18 weeks gestation. All of the abnormalities listed above are forms of neural tube defects and therefore would be expected to have an elevated alpha-fetoprotein level, except for subarachnoid hemorrhage.

ANSWER 32

C. The above infant presents with evidence of malabsorption with the chronic diarrhea and poor weight gain. He also has eczema and blood in the stools, which are often associated with a milk allergy. Twenty-five percent of patients with a milk protein allergy are also intolerant of a soy formula. The allergy is to the milk protein, not the sugar, lactose. The treatment of choice would be breastfeeding for the first year of life. The mother should be careful to remove whole milk from her diet. If unable to breast feed and the patient is intolerant to soy, a hydrolysated casein formula, such as Nutramigen or Pregestimil, should be started.

A. Genetically inherited lactose intolerance may produce abdominal distention, fussiness, and watery stools. However, this patient's symptoms progressed on a soy formula, which does not contain lactose.

B. Milk protein intolerance is often mistaken for colic. However, an infant with colic would continue to feed and grow normally.

D. Gastroesophageal reflux may cause fussiness and frequent spit ups, and if severe enough, esophagitis, and poor weight gain. However, reflux usually does not cause abdominal distention and watery stools.

E. Necrotizing enterocolitis does present with acute abdominal distention and bloody stools, but it is an acute process that rarely presents in a one-and-a-half-month-old patient with a normal birth history.

ANSWER 33

B. Congenital cataract is the most common cause of leukocoria in an otherwise healthy, full term newborn. The other choices are all other causes of leukocoria or a white pupil.

A. Retinoblastoma should always be considered in the differential of an asymmetric red reflex. Although uncommon, this diagnosis requires early intervention.

C. Retinopathy of prematurity is not seen in full term infants.

D. Congenital glaucoma is an uncommon but important diagnosis in infants with an asymmetric red reflex. Tearing, irritability, and a large pupil may also be seen.

E. Ocular toxoplasmosis may occur in infants with maternal exposure to *Toxoplasma gondii*. Infants with severe disease may have chorioretinitis, intracranial calcifications, and mental retardation.

ANSWER 34

C. Obesity, prepubertal age, and male gender are associated with the diagnosis of slipped capital femoral epiphysis. It is also associated with hormonal abnormalities, including hypothyroidism, growth hormone deficiency, and decreased levels of estrogen or testosterone. Management of this patient requires an orthopedic evaluation and possible casting or surgical treatment.

A. Only 25% or less lose their obesity with adolescence.

B. Knee pain may be referred from a hip problem.

D. Obesity is associated with many serious health problems and is important to treat, but diet will not be enough in this case.

E. This may be true, but now he has a complication from the obesity and needs immediate referral and treatment.

ANSWER 35

D. This patient has mild persistent asthma and is requiring use of her rescue beta2-agonist more than twice a week. An inhaled low dose steroid is the first line of therapy in controlling her symptoms.

A. There is nothing in the history provided that describes allergic symptoms that would be better controlled with an antihistamine.

B. Cromolyn sodium is sometimes used in addition to beta2-agonists, but inhaled steroids are first line therapy.

C. Theophylline is no longer preferred therapy because of side effects and drug levels that need to be followed.

E. Daily prednisone is used only in severe persistent asthmatics that are on maximum therapy and still having symptoms.

ANSWER 36

B. Torsion is much more common than orchitis in childhood and this should be kept in mind when considering the diagnosis of testicular pain.

A. Elevation of the testicle results in pain relief.

C. Only a few hours remain for intervention before irreversible damage occurs.

D. Orchitis is caused by viral infections, which would not respond to antibiotic treatment.

E. As mumps is a primary cause of orchitis, the widespread use of this vaccine has decreased the number of cases of orchitis.

ANSWER 37

A. Two-year-old children usually produce 2–3 word phrases, may follow 2-step commands, and be understood by a stranger about 50% of the time.

B. See explanation for A.

C. Speech therapy is not necessary and should not be offered as an option.

D. Speech therapy is not necessary.

E. ENT clinic is unnecessary.

ANSWER 38

C. Eisenmenger physiology results from excess pulmonary vascular resistance and subsequent right ventricular enlargement and failure. This is usually seen in the context of a large VSD, in which the left-to-right shunt has flooded the pulmonary circulation. Over time this results in elevated pulmonary vascular resistance, and the ventricular shunt reverses to a right-to-left shunt which results in cyanosis. The clinical presentation described above is that of increased pulmonary vascular resistance and right-to-left shunt characteristic of Eisenmenger's syndrome.

ANSWER 39

C. A thoracic duct injury, in which chyle leaks into the chest cavity, is a relatively common complication after neonatal repair of congenital cardiac disease.

A. A hemothorax would not have milky fluid on thoracentesis.

B. Parenteral nutrition is delivered via venous access, usually in a large vein (subclavian, femoral). If there were venous rupture in the thorax, the fluid obtained would be bloody.

D. A post-op pneumonia causing a parapneumonic effusion would tend to be clear to slightly blood tinged.

E. A hydrothorax would not have milky fluid and generally is associated with edema or fluid in other parts of the body. Causes include hepatic, cardiac, or renal failure.

ANSWER 40

D. Moisturizing skin and anti-inflammatory creams are the mainstay of treatment to minimize the drying and itching, which cause the rash.

A. Bathing dries the skin and worsens eczema.

B. Allergy tests correlate poorly with eczema and allergy shots have not been proven in the treatment of eczema.

C. This type of dietary restriction is not helpful and may result in nutritional deficiencies.

E. Oral steroids will clear the rash, but the result is only temporary, and long-term use would risk steroid dependency and immune suppression.

ANSWER 41

D. Thelarche or the appearance of breast buds is the first event in puberty in females. Following thelarche are the height growth spurt, pubic hair, growth, and menarche. Voice change is not an event in female sexual development.

ANSWER 42

E. All of the above abnormalities are associated with diabetes insipidus (DI), which may occur post-operatively during surgery involving the pituitary stalk. In DI, there is an absence of anti-diuretic hormone from the posterior pituitary gland, and therefore there is an inability to concentrate the urine. Excess free water is lost, causing a dilute high-volume urine output and subsequent hemoconcentration and hypernatremia.

ANSWER 43

E. The child has what appears to be consistent with hemolytic uremic syndrome due to uncooked or infected beef. The infant is in acute renal failure with an elevated creatinine and potassium. Fluids should be given very cautiously due to the inability of the kidneys to remove excess fluid, leading to pulmonary edema.

A. Patients with acute renal failure may have multiple EKG abnormalities, including T-wave elevations, loss of P-waves, a widened QRS, and S-T depression.

B. Intensive monitoring is recommended until potassium levels are in a safe range.

C. Calcium gluconate is used to help stabilize the cardiac cell membrane.

D. Insulin and glucose drive potassium into the cells, decreasing serum levels.

ANSWER 44

D. The duration of the symptoms, history of being an "A" student, and type A competitive personality all make chronic abdominal pain most likely. As stress is internalized and somaticized, stress often is not shown outwardly.

A. The history is too chronic to be typical for appendicitis.

B. There is no history of diarrhea or blood in the stools, and no history of bloating/gaseous pain.

C. IBD tends to have a more chronic history of diarrhea with blood in the stools and progressive worsening of the disease.

E. Gallbladder disease is unlikely in pediatrics unless there is a history of hemoglobinopathy, chronic TPN, or other underlying illnesses.

ANSWER 45

B. Acute lymphocytic leukemia (ALL) is the most common form of childhood malignancy. The age of the child is important in evaluating the prognosis in a specific case and is an important factor in choosing the appropriate chemotherapeutic regimen. Children less than 2 years of age or greater than 10 years of age are at much higher risk than children between the ages of 2 and 10. This child's age of 6 years places him in a favorable prognostic category.

A. The male sex is an unfavorable or high risk factor in childhood ALL.

C. The cell morphology is critical in evaluating prognosis and treatment decision. The L1 morphology is the most favorable cell type in childhood ALL. L2 and L3 morphologies are unfavorable as is PAS negative staining.

D. A very low platelet count (<100,000) is an unfavorable finding in this case. Very low (<10,000) or very high (>50,000) white blood counts are also high risk factors.

E. The hemoglobin levels >10 g/dl in this case is an unfavorable prognostic factor.

ANSWER 46

E. This photograph shows a scalp defect, or cutis aplasia, a common feature of trisomy 13 syndrome. This condition is associated with an extremely poor prognosis for survival. Thirty percent of patients die by one month of age, and 90% die by one year. The few who survive beyond that age are severely mentally retarded.

A. Trisomy 13 is a chromosome disorder, not a single gene disorder.

B. Trisomy 13 may be easily diagnosed prenatally by either amniocentesis or chorionic villus sampling (CVS).

C. Trisomy 13 is usually caused by an extra copy of chromosome 13. Usually this occurs *de novo* by nondisjunction, but one-fourth of cases are familial, due to a parental chromosome translocation.

D. Both males and females are equally affected; this condition does not cause lethality in males.

ANSWER 47

C. This school-age child has an atypical pneumonia with erythema multiforme, which is consistent with mycoplasma pneumonia infections. Mycoplasma is the most common cause of atypical pneumonias in school-aged children.

A. *Streptococcus pneumoniae* is the most common cause of typical bacterial pneumonia in children. Patients usually are tachypneic and febrile with a consolidated lobar infiltrate on chest x-ray.

B. *Chlamydia pneumoniae* may cause interstitial, atypical pneumonias. Patients are usually afebrile. There is no association with erythema multiforme. See Answer A.

D. *Haemophilus influenzae* is a cause of bacterial pneumonia in children, again with a consolidated lobar infiltrate.

E. Influenza A may cause a viral pneumonia with interstitial infiltrates, but patients typically have systemic symptoms such as fever, malaise, and myalgias.

ANSWER 48

D. For lead levels over 45 µg/dl, chelation treatment is usually needed. If oral chelation with succimer is used as an outpatient, there must be assurance that the home environment is free of lead.

A. A repeat lead level within 3 months is acceptable for children with lead levels between 10 and 14 µg/dl, but is not adequate management for a lead level this high. Action should be taken within 48 hours.

B. A complete investigation must be done to identify whether or not the home is actually the source of lead. It is less common for a house built as late as 1980 to contain lead paint. Lead can also come from pottery, soil, home remedies, plumbing, and automobile repair supplies, batteries, and various solvents.

C. Any patient who has a blood lead level over 20 µg/dl needs careful evaluation and repeated blood lead levels.

E. Emergency hospitalization and intravenous chelation is usually reserved for children with lead levels over 70 µg/dl.

ANSWER 49

C. Due to the alteration of blood flow and vasoconstriction associated with cocaine, these infants are at increased risk of early onset NEC.

A. These neonates are frequently small for gestational age (SGA) since cocaine is a powerful anorexic in the mothers. It also acts as a potent vasoconstrictor and frequently produces placental insufficiency.

B. Cocaine-exposed infants have a 3–7 times higher risk for SIDS.

D. Cocaine is a common cause of preterm labor and spontaneous abortions.

E. Cocaine-addicted neonates may have abnormal sleep patterns with an inability to be consoled.

ANSWER 50

A. The patient described in the clinical vignette most likely has petit mal or absence seizures. The characteristic EEG pattern for these seizures is the generalized, symmetric 3-per-second spike and wave pattern. Petit mal or absence seizures are brief, repetitive episodes associated with alterations in consciousness, and the child is unaware of the episodes. There is usually no post-ictal period and the child quickly returns to the task at hand. Hypsarryhthmia is the characteristic EEG pattern seen in infantile spasma. The two other EEG patterns listed are not specific for any particular disorder.

BLOCK TWO

ANSWERS

ANSWER 51

E. This adolescent has gonococcal pelvic inflammatory disease. She has evidence of cervicitis with systemic symptoms including fever and abdominal pain.

A. A normal urinalysis in the absence of dysuria, suprapubic tenderness, and cervical motion tenderness virtually excludes pyelonephritis.

B. No right lower quadrant pain or peritoneal signs on examination make this diagnosis unlikely. However, appendicitis should always be considered in patients with fever and lower abdominal pain.

C. With no adnexal mass and a negative serum HCG, it is an unlikely diagnosis.

D. Endometriosis causes chronic, intermittent pelvic and/or abdominal pain, but not fever and vaginal discharge.

ANSWER 52

A. Successful treatment depends on early recognition and referral for occlusion therapy.

B. It is important to monitor the amount of television exposure, but this alone is not a root cause of amblyopia.

C. Although recent reports show there may be some small benefit even from late treatment, corrective therapy is most successful prior to 8 years of age.

D. Treatment of amblyopia may include occlusion of the "good eye," forcing the child to use the "bad" or lazy eye.

E. Some of the known risk factors for amblyopia include strabismus, myopia, muscle weakness, cataract.

ANSWER 53

D. Shoulder dystocia with large infants is commonly associated with clavicular fracture. Fractures occur when the shoulders are compressed between the sacrum and the symphysis pubis, or with arms or shoulders extended during breech delivery.

A. Fractures of the clavicle are the most common neonatal fracture, occurring in from 2–7 per 1,000 live births even with excellent obstetrical care.

B. Brachial plexus injury and pneumothorax is very uncommon.

C. Healing normally progresses over several months, first with callous formation followed by remodeling.

E. This injury is usually benign but is occasionally associated with a pneumothorax or brachial plexus injury. Neither would be treated by an orthopedist. Treatment is supportive to decrease pain in the infant by avoiding positioning the infant on the injured side and immobilizing the arm until discomfort has resolved.

ANSWER 54

D. This patient has continual daytime and frequent nighttime symptoms despite good medical therapy. His PEF is <60%, which classifies him as severe persistent. He may benefit from addition of low dose daily or every other day oral steroids to try and control his symptoms.

A. Mild intermittent has daily symptoms <2x/week and nighttime symptoms <2x/month. Their PEF is >80%.

B. Mild persistent has daytime symptoms 3–6x/week and nighttime symptoms 3–4x/month. Their PEF is <80%.

C. Moderate persistent has daily daytime symptoms with nighttime symptoms occurring >5x/month. Their PEF is >60% and <80%.

ANSWER 55

C. Obstruction of the nasolacrimal duct is a common cause of overflow tearing (epiphora) in neonates. The most common cause of obstruction is a persistent membrane that blocks the distal end of the nasolacrimal duct where it empties into the nose.

A. Dacryocystitis is a superimposed infection of the tear duct.

B. Open globe implies rupture of the sclera and is uncommon.

D. An uncommon cause of painless tearing in a baby.

E. An uncommon cause of painless tearing in a baby.

ANSWER 56

A. The patient described above has an exam consistent with aortic stenosis. Symptoms are often absent even if obstruction is severe. The patient should not be allowed to participate in sports, as sudden death has been reported. An echocardiogram should be performed to assess the valvular lesion, the degree of the stenosis, and the left ventricular function. All of these factors will determine the appropriate intervention to repair or replace the valve. Patients with this valvular lesion should receive antibiotic prophylaxis to prevent bacterial endocarditis when undergoing dental manipulation or instrumentation of the gastrointestinal or genitourinary tract.

ANSWER 57

C. Hyponatremia from the syndrome of inappropriate secretion of ADH (SIADH) is a common complication of bacterial meningitis. Hyponatremic seizures are notoriously resistant to anticonvulsants and need to be treated with appropriate saline solutions.

A. A brain abscess is a complication that may cause seizures, but usually is not one of the presenting signs. This complication may need neurosurgical care.

B. Again, subdural empyema is not a presenting sign, but seizures resulting from irritation from an empyema usually respond well to therapy.

D. Increased ICP is a possible complication from meningitis and may cause seizures. Medical therapy is usually not sufficient.

E. This child is too old to make a diagnosis of a febrile seizure. Given the presenting signs and symptoms one should always consider bacterial infection first.

ANSWER 58

D. Roseola is characterized by 3 days of high fever, which disappears suddenly as the typical rash appears.

A. Rubella is typically only a 3-day illness and the rash would already be present.

B. Children are unlikely to have fever with erythema infectiosum.

C. Erythema toxicum is a common normal newborn rash.

E. This diagnosis is unlikely because the child is acting well between fevers and does not appear toxic; he is also not seriously ill after a 3-day history of illness.

ANSWER 59

C. The milestones above are appropriate for a child of 15 months. At this age a child should be able to walk backwards, creep up stairs, scribble, build a tower of two blocks, and use 4–6 words.

A. At 9 months, the average child can neither walk nor talk.

B. An average 1-year-old knows 1–3 words and cannot walk backwards.

D. At 2 years, a child should know about 100 words and be able to walk up and down stairs.

E. At 3 years, a child should be able to use 3-word sentences, dress himself, and draw a circle.

ANSWER 60

B. Rickets is a cause of disproportionate short stature. This condition predominantly affects the long bones and results in disproportionate growth of the extremities compared with the trunk.

A. Malnutrition is commonly associated with proportionate short stature.

C. Teratogen exposure, intrauterine growth retardation, and placental dysfunction are prenatal causes of proportionate short stature.

D. Turner's syndrome and trisomy 21 are chromosomal causes of proportionate short stature.

E. Constitutional delay is one of the most common causes of proportionate short stature.

ANSWER 61

E. Nephrotic syndrome is a common cause of edema in pediatric patients. Eighty-five percent of patients have minimal change disease on renal biopsy. The majority of patients respond to prednisone. Red blood cell casts are commonly seen in tubular disease or nephritis.

A. Proteinuria is a hallmark of nephrotic syndrome.

B. Hypoalbuminemia occurs as a result of large protein losses in the urine.

C. Edema of the face, extremities, and ascites may develop as protein losses increase.

D. Triglycerides are typically protein bound and serum levels of triglycerides will increase as protein losses increase.

ANSWER 62

C. Gastroesophageal reflux is due to an incompetent lower esophageal sphincter and is worsened by feeding while lying down. Emesis from reflux is not projectile and does not contain bilious material. Complications include aspiration, poor weight gain, esophagitis, and apneic episodes.

A. Pyloric stenosis is four times more common in males, causes "projectile" emesis, and is associated with a palpable olive-like mass or visible peristalsis.

B. Emesis in volvulus is generally bilious.

D. Gastroenteritis implies concomitant diarrhea and often fever.

E. The volume of emesis and the association with the baby lying on her back are more consistent with reflux.

ANSWER 63

C. This child has a history that is typical of iron deficiency anemia. Large amounts of cow's milk intake, as seen with this child, often result in chronic blood loss in the stool. While iron is absorbed very well from breast milk, feeding of other foods will decrease this absorption. Whole milk does not have adequate amounts of iron. Babies should continue an iron containing formula until 12 months of age. Following the initiation of oral iron, the reticulocyte count will begin to rise in about 10 days and the hemoglobin will be markedly improved by 4 weeks. If these responses are not seen, other diagnoses or compliance problems must be considered. A low serum ferritin demonstrates poor body iron stores.

A. This child requires oral iron immediately.

B. While lead poisoning often coexists with iron deficiency, the home does not need to be checked at this time.

D. Children who have no cardiorespiratory symptoms do not require transfusion.

E. Dietary changes are not adequate treatment for this degree of anemia.

ANSWER 64

D. This patient has Turner's syndrome, which is not typically associated with central nervous system malformations or mental retardation, although they may have some mild learning disabilities. Lymphedema of the hands and feet at birth is common in Turner's syndrome. Cystic hygroma is very common in Turner's and may lead to hydrops fetalis and death in utero. When it resolves, webbing of the neck skin may be seen.

A. Congenital heart disease occurs in 20% of patients with Turner's syndrome, most commonly coarctation of the aorta, aortic stenosis, and bicuspid aortic valve.

B. Renal anomalies are seen in 40% of patients with Turner's syndrome, most commonly horseshoe kidney.

C. Turner's syndrome is diagnosed by chromosome analysis. The most common karyotype is 45, X (60%). X chromosome abnormalities account for another 25% of cases, and 15% of patients have a mosaic karyotype, which may include a Y chromosome cell line.

E. Short stature and gonadal dysgenesis are typical in Turner's syndrome. Growth hormone therapy is standard of care to improve height and oral estrogen/progesterone are used to induce secondary sexual characteristics, although most patients are sterile.

ANSWER 65

B. Mastoiditis presents clinically as described above. CT scan will reveal clouding to destruction of septa between mastoid cells with soft tissue swelling behind the affected ear. Temporal bone destruction may also be seen along with soft tissue abscesses.

A. With acute otitis media, you would expect to see some free fluid around the ossicles when a suppurative effusion is present. This is also seen with mastoiditis. See Answer B.

C. Clear mastoid cells with surrounding free fluid of the ossicles is consistent with acute otitis media.

D. In patients with clinical mastoiditis, you would not expect to have a normal CT scan.

ANSWER 66

D. This toddler has a foreign body aspiration, as suggested by his lung and CXR findings. A foreign body should always be considered in the differential of a wheezing toddler. Management includes removal under direct visualization by rigid bronchoscopy.

A. Beta agonist therapy is appropriate for the management of asthma.

B. Steroid therapy is used for the management of asthma exacerbation and is not useful in the treatment of a foreign body aspiration.

C. Chest tube placement is indicated for lung collapse, as opposed to hyperinflation.

E. Racemic epinephrine is used in the treatment of laryngotracheobronchitis (croup) and is indicated in patients with stridor at rest.

ANSWER 67

D. Hearing loss is the most common sequela of congenital CMV infections and should be screened for as soon as the diagnosis is entertained.

A. Acute fulminant CMV infections in the neonate present with multiorgan involvement. CMV affects the liver presenting with elevated direct bilirubin and transaminases. It also causes hepatosplenomegaly with petechiae related to abnormal spleen sequestration and thrombocytopenia.

B. Periventricular calcifications are a classic finding on head ultrasound or CT of the head with congenital CMV infections, but calcifications may occur anywhere in the brain.

C. Mental retardation is common and related to both microcephaly, central nervous system calcifications, and neurologic dysfunction from primary CMV infection.

E. Microcephaly is not specific for congenital CMV infections but may be seen in up to 15% of patients.

ANSWER 68

D. The clinical description of the child above most closely fits the neurocutaneous disorder known as tuberous sclerosis. This is a progressive, autosomal dominant disorder characterized by ash-leaf spots (flat, hypopigmented macules), shagreen patches (areas of abnormal skin thickening), sebaceous adenomas (sometimes confused with acne), and hyperpigmented macules on the forehead. Mental retardation and seizures usually accompany the cutaneous manifestations, and neuroimaging demonstrates distinctive periventricular "tubers."

A. Sturge–Weber syndrome is characterized by port-wine lesions on the face in the distribution of the trigeminal nerve and is associated with vascular proliferation within the brain leading to hemiatrophy and seizures, as well as vascular proliferation in the eye which may lead to glaucoma.

B. Von Hippel–Lindau disease is characterized by vascular hamartomas in the eye and brain and is associated with renal cell tumors and pheochromocytoma.

C. Neurofibromatosis is characterized by multiple café-au-lait macules on the skin as well as the development of fibromas. It is also associated with hypertension secondary to renal artery stenosis.

ANSWER 69

A. Fever is a minor criterion. The five major criteria are chorea, carditis, erythema marginatum, subcutaneous nodules, and migratory polyarthritis. The diagnosis of rheumatic fever requires the presence of either two major criteria, or one major criterion and two minor criteria, plus evidence of an antecedent streptococcal infection (throat culture, rapid antigen test or elevated or increasing streptococcal antibody test). Minor criteria include fever, arthralgia, prolonged PR interval, and elevation of acute phase reactants.

B. Sydenham's chorea occurs in 10–15% of patients with acute rheumatic fever (ARF).

C. This is the most serious manifestation of ARF characterized by pancarditis. Endocarditis affecting the aortic and mitral valves can lead to acute regurgitation and long-term valvular stenosis.

D. Occurs in <3% of patients with ARF. It consists of erythematous macular lesions with pale centers that are not pruritic. It occurs primarily on the trunk and extremities, not the face.

E. Occurs in <1% of patients with ARF. Approximately 1 cm nodules may be palpated along extensor tendon surfaces and correlates with significant rheumatic heart disease.

ANSWER 70

E. Frequent infections do not present a high risk for eye pathology.

A. Family history of amblyopia is a risk factor for amblyopia.

B. Premature infants are at risk for retinopathy of prematurity.

C. Patients with cerebral palsy are at risk for strabismus.

D. Maternal intrauterine TORCH infections may result in cataracts or chorioretinitis.

ANSWER 71

C. Most of these children are healthy infants with a clubfoot of unknown cause and will crawl, stand, and walk. Untreated, this condition may result in severe disability and deformity.

A. Rigid clubfoot may respond to manipulation and casting. However, if these interventions fail, surgery will be required.

B. Most cases are idiopathic and have no other associated abnormalities.

D. Very early intervention may produce a shorter treatment period, but if conservative treatment fails (casting), surgery may be required followed by casting and bracing. Patients must then be followed for any evidence of recurrence.

E. Even with successful treatment, the foot may be smaller and possibly less mobile than the normal foot; however, most children will still be able to participate fully in normal activities.

ANSWER 72

E. See individual descriptions below.

A. Rectal prolapse occurs in up to 20% of patients with cystic fibrosis. It is related to the passage of large bulky stools from pancreatic insufficiency and improves when patients are placed on pancreatic enzyme replacement.

B. Protein-calorie malnutrition or failure to thrive occurs because of fat malabsorption and the need for increased caloric intake. Some patients need 120–140% of daily-recommended caloric intake to grow and gain weight.

C. Nasal polyps are common in cystic fibrosis patients with chronic sinopulmonary disease and may be seen in young infants.

D. Almost all post pubertal males are infertile secondary to obstructive azoospermia.

ANSWER 73

D. Toys may attract children to the pool area. Children may also stand on large toys, chairs, and tables in order to climb over the fence to get into the pool.

A. The American Academy of Pediatrics does not recommend swimming lessons for infants. There is no scientific evidence to prove young infants can be "drownproofed."

B. Children who drown in residential pools often sink quickly and make almost no noise.

C. Careful supervision is key to drowning prevention, but proper pool fencing has been shown to be effective. A pool should be fenced on all four sides to prevent access from doors and windows at the back of the house. The gate should be self-closing and self-latching.

E. Bathtub support rings are not effective. Small children should never be left alone in a bathtub. Babies have even drowned in large buckets containing a small amount of liquid.

ANSWER 74

A. The hyperoxia test is used as an early tool to evaluate the cyanotic neonate to determine if the etiology of the cyanosis is cardiac or non-cardiac in origin. A right radial artery (preductal) blood gas is performed with the child inspiring room air and 100% oxygen. The change in PaO_2 with the administration of oxygen issued as a guide to determine the etiology of the cyanosis. A PaO_2 of less than 150 with the administration of 100% oxygen suggests a cardiac lesion. The cardiac lesions may be further classified based upon the absolute value of the PaO_2. A PaO_2 of less than 50 on 100% oxygen suggests a cardiac disorder, in which there is restricted pulmonary blood flow or a separate venous and arterial circulation, whereas a PaO_2 between 50 and 150 on 100% oxygen suggests that there is no restriction of pulmonary blood flow in the presence of complete mixing of oxygenated and deoxygenated blood. In this case, the PaO_2 on 100% oxygen was less than 50, suggesting restricted pulmonary blood flow or a separate circulation.

ANSWER 75

B. Skin care in sepsis-associated purpura fulminans is an important part of therapy. Topical antibiotics may be used for open areas, but blisters should not be unroofed because these are at high risk for secondary infection.

A. Broad-spectrum empiric antibiotic therapy is appropriate until the etiology is firm (i.e., results from blood culture available). Numerous bacterial agents have been associated with purpura fulminans.

C. Isolation is required for patients presenting with purpura fulminans.

D. Treatment of sepsis-associated purpura fulminans is directed against the underlying etiology as well as shock. An initial step is LR or NS boluses.

E. Blood cultures are important in the diagnosis of this disease. While they should never delay antibiotics, they are often positive in sepsis-associated purpura fulminans and may be used to narrow antibiotic coverage.

ANSWER 76

C. This presentation is consistent with a capillary hemangioma, which is not uncommon in infants. They often develop shortly after birth, increase in size over the first year of life, then involute over several years. They usually disappear by age 8–10 years. They should be treated only if they are excessively large or in vital areas (eyelid, airway, vaginal). Treatments include excision, steroids, laser treatment, or interferon.

A. Punch biopsy is unnecessary and could be dangerous due to heavy bleeding.

B. These lesions are benign but usually grow larger over the first year, then gradually involute.

D. Steroid injection is not necessary in most cases.

E. This is not an infectious lesion and antibiotics would be unhelpful.

ANSWER 77

A. Sensorimotor stage is the correct answer. This stage encompasses birth to 2 years of age and consists of children learning by activity, explanation, and manipulation of the environment.

B. Preoperational stage, ages 2–7: the child engages in symbolic representation of the world.

C. Concrete operation, ages 7–11: the child is capable of limited, logical thought process.

D. Abstract operations is not a stage of Piaget's cognitive development.

E. Formal operations, ages 12 to adult: the child can reason logically and abstractly.

ANSWER 78

A. Children with constitutional delay grow and develop at or below the fifth percentile, but have normal growth velocities. Puberty is significantly delayed, which results in delayed skeletal maturation and a delayed bone age. There is often a family history of short stature in childhood and delayed puberty.

B. Children with familial short stature have a normal bone age and puberty is not delayed.

C. Primary hypothyroidism results in a diminished growth velocity.

D. Children with growth hormone deficiency will have a delayed bone age and will show growth well below the third percentile. These children will also have a diminished growth velocity.

E. Children with chronic systemic diseases may develop short stature either from a lack of calorie absorption or from calorie depletion from increased metabolic demands. Their growth velocity is abnormal, and there is marked retardation of bone age and pubertal delay.

ANSWER 79

D. Hypernatremic dehydration is seen in about 10–15% of patients with dehydration. The serum sodium level should be lowered slowly, no faster than 10–12 milliequivalents in 24 hours, due to the risk of cerebral edema and seizures.

A. Subdural hematomas may occur due to intracellular fluid loss.

B. Hypernatremia may be seen with improperly mixed formulas.

C. 20cc/kg normal saline or lactated ringers fluid boluses should be given until the infant is clinically stable.

E. Hypernatremia is seen in 10–15% of patients.

ANSWER 80

D. To make the diagnosis of failure to thrive (FTT), it is important to plot height and weight on standard growth curve and especially important to compare these to previous values if they are known. FTT refers to growth <3rd or 5th %ile on >1 occasion in a child <2 years old; a child <2 years whose weight is <80% of the ideal weight for age; or a child <2 years whose weight crosses two major percentiles.

A. According to the history, this child is meeting his developmental milestones appropriately.

B. This is an important component of an FTT workup, but FTT must be established first.

C. The child's previous illnesses are minor and would not result in growth problems or warrant an immune workup.

E. Cystic fibrosis is one cause of FTT, but this is not the initial step.

ANSWER 81

D. This patient has idiopathic thrombocytopenic purpura (ITP), a condition that often follows viral infection or immunization. Most cases resolve spontaneously without therapy. Parents should be advised that children should not engage in activities that increase their risk for injury or bleeding. Aspirin and ibuprofen should be avoided. Parents need to be reassured that most children with ITP get better within 2–3 months.

A. Platelet transfusions are indicated only in cases of life threatening bleeding.

B. Experts disagree on whether or not to give steroids for children with platelet counts less than 20,000. Bleeding is not generally a problem with a platelet count of 45,000.

C. This child does not require admission to an intensive care unit for observation.

E. Spontaneous bleeding mostly occurs in the first two weeks of illness. As with steroids, IVIG is not indicated in a child with a platelet count of 45,000.

ANSWER 82

C. This boy has fragile X syndrome, an X-linked disorder caused by expansion of a trinucleotide repeat region in the FMR-1 gene on chromosome Xq. Mothers of affected patients are obligate gene carriers with an intermediate size gene expansion and may have mild learning and behavior problems.

A. Both parents are gene carriers only in autosomal recessive conditions.

B. Boys with fragile X syndrome have normal genitalia and may develop macroorchidism at puberty.

D. In an X-linked condition, there is a 50% recurrence risk for brothers to be affected, but a much lesser risk for sisters.

E. Fragile X chromosome analysis will reveal a "fragile site" on one X chromosome, not an extra chromosome. DNA analysis of the CGG repeat region of the FMR-1 gene is now the preferred testing method.

ANSWER 83

B. Palivizumab should be given monthly during RSV season only to infants/children who meet specific criteria. Palivizumab is approved for prevention of RSV disease in children younger than 24 months of age with bronchopulmonary dysplasia or with a history of premature birth (<35 weeks gestation). It should be considered for use in infants and children younger than 2 years of age with chronic lung disease who have required medical therapy within 6 months before the RSV season.

A. It is a humanized mouse monoclonal antibody.

C. It is NOT FDA approved for infants/children with congenital heart disease.

D. An infant with severe prematurity <28 weeks gestation at birth will benefit from prophylaxis.

E. Any infant with chronic lung disease currently or in the last 6 months requiring O_2 meets criteria for prophylaxis.

ANSWER 84

D. A workup for suspected nonaccidental trauma should include a careful history to determine if the explanation is consistent with the nature and degree of the injury and consistent with the developmental age of the child. Skeletal radiographs to look for old and new fractures are important. Retinal hemorrhages may be associated with shaken baby syndrome. Clotting disorders should be ruled out in children with bruising.

A. A confrontational approach may cause the mother to flee the emergency department with the baby. It is important to remain calm and carry out the evaluation in a professional manner.

B. Unless associated with intracranial hemorrhage, linear skull fractures are generally not associated with severe brain damage.

C. This child does not have a medical condition that warrants admission to an intensive care unit. In fact, if a safe home environment can be assured, hospital admission may not be necessary.

E. In cases of suspected child abuse, the baby should not be sent home until the Child Protective Services agency has completed an evaluation and determined the home setting to be safe.

ANSWER 85

C. An intraventricular hemorrhage with ventricular dilatation is a grade 3 hemorrhage.

A. Grade 1 is an isolated subependymal hemorrhage. Most are asymptomatic.

B. Grade 2 is an intraventricular hemorrhage without ventricular dilatation.

D. Grade 4 is an intraventricular hemorrhage with parenchymal extension and has the worst overall prognosis.

ANSWER 86

B. Status epilepticus is a dangerous condition which may lead to hypoxia and brain damage if not treated expeditiously. The airway, breathing, and circulation should be evaluated and any abnormalities corrected. Intravenous or rectal administration of a benzodiazepine is very effective in breaking the seizure cycle. A loading dose of phenytoin is usually administered to prevent recurrences. Neuroimaging tests should not be done until the seizure activity is under control and may not be necessary in a patient with a chronic seizure disorder. A thorough evaluation should be performed after the prolonged seizure is controlled and then the need for neuroimaging tests may be determined.

ANSWER 87

B. Thalassemia trait is often confused with iron deficiency because both conditions are associated with microcytic anemia. In heterozygous beta thalassemia, the hemoglobin electrophoresis will show elevations of hemoglobin A2 and hemoglobin F. No treatment is needed, but genetic counseling is recommended.

A. The child's diet does not have excess milk ingestion to suggest a dietary cause of iron deficiency anemia and there is nothing in the history to suggest blood loss. Iron deficiency would also be expected to improve significantly after a month of treatment.

C. Anemia is never normal in 2-year-old children.

D. A transfusion is necessary when anemic children have signs of cardiac decompensation. This child has no such symptoms.

E. Poor compliance with oral iron therapy is common and could explain the lack of improvement in hemoglobin level in this patient. If compliance is being questioned, a serum ferritin level to check body iron stores would be valuable. The ferritin would be low in iron deficiency, but normal in homozygous thalassemia.

ANSWER 88

D. Tears are generally not produced before 3 weeks of age, and therefore a blocked nasolacrimal duct usually becomes apparent after one month of age.

A. Chlamydia and gonorrhea are the most common ocular infections in neonates.

B. Herpes simplex virus is less common than bacterial eye infections, but may present after 5 days of age.

C. Chemical irritation is the cause of 80% of red eyes in neonates.

E. *Staphylococcus aureus* is also a cause of neonatal eye infections.

ANSWER 89

D. Buckle or torus fractures are stable injuries commonly treated with a short or long arm cast for 3–6 weeks with an excellent prognosis. Nonunion is rare in uncomplicated cases of buckle fracture.

A. Forearm fractures account for about one-fourth of all children's fractures.

B. Rotation or angulation of forearm fracture requires more complex management and follow-up with a higher risk of complications.

C. This is the classic mechanism of injury in children.

E. Buckle fractures are commonly incomplete (greenstick) but may be complete in more severe cases.

ANSWER 90

B. The chest x-ray in pulmonary hemosiderosis usually reveals diffuse fluffy infiltrates, secondary to alveolar hemorrhaging. Lung biopsy typically reveals alveolar hemorrhages with hemosiderin laden macrophages.

A. Blood-tinged sputum is associated with coughing secondary to alveolar hemorrhaging.

C. Some cases of pulmonary hemosiderosis are associated with a milk allergy. This is called Heiner syndrome. Many of these children may have upper airway obstruction. Milk products should be eliminated as part of therapy.

D. Lung biopsy typically reveals alveolar hemorrhages with hemosiderin laden macrophages.

E. Iron deficiency anemia may be present secondary to the chronic pulmonary hemorrhaging.

ANSWER 91

B. Burns with sharp margins should raise a suspicion of abuse. A child who steps into hot water with one foot would not place the second foot into the hot bath water. The stocking distribution is seen when a child is intentionally "dipped" into hot water, often as punishment.

A. Getting medical care soon after an injury demonstrates parental concern. Seeking care long after an injury may raise suspicion for abuse.

C. Scald burns may be the result of intentional or unintentional mechanisms. In fact, scalds are the most common type of burns in childhood.

D. Splash burns are often the result of unintentional injury.

E. Many good caring parents do not know that hot water heater temperatures should be set below 125 degrees to minimize the chance of unintentional scald burns. Most Child Protective Service agencies would not consider this child neglect.

ANSWER 92

A. I.M. Ceftriaxone is considered adequate prophylaxis for meningococcus and is often preferred in the pregnant woman.

B. Four doses of rifampin given 12 hours apart are considered adequate prophylaxis for meningococcus.

C. Terminal complement studies are ordered for patients with recurrent disease to rule out complement deficiencies, as these patients are more susceptible to meningococcal disease.

D. The meningococcal vaccine is given to those patients who are without a spleen, are functionally asplenic (sickle cell), have a terminal complement deficiency, are living in a dormitory environment, or are in the midst of an epidemic.

E. Respiratory isolation may be discontinued after 24 hours of appropriate antibiotic therapy.

ANSWER 93

A. Asthma is the most common chronic illness of childhood. This child has eczema/atopic dermatitis. Children with allergies and/or eczema are at an increased risk for developing asthma compared to the general population.

ANSWER 94

D. This is the correct order of sexual maturation in males.

A. This is the reverse order.

B. Penile enlargement occurs after testicular enlargement.

C. Pubic hair growth is the last step of sexual maturation.

ANSWER 95

A. Oral rehydration therapy is the preferable treatment for mild to moderate dehydration. The World Health Organization (WHO) rehydration solution contains 90 milliequivalents of sodium per liter, 20 milliequivalents of potassium per liter, and 20 g of glucose per liter.

B. Intraosseous access is obtained when intravenous access cannot be obtained.

C. Lumbar puncture is performed and antibiotics are given when sepsis is suspected.

D. Fruit juice may exacerbate diarrhea.

E. This patient does not require inpatient care at this time.

ANSWER 96

D. This child has Kawasaki disease as characterized by the nonexudative conjunctival injection, polymorphous nonvesicular rash, mucosal involvement, edema of the hands and feet, and cervical lymphadenopathy. Due to the cardiac complications (coronary aneurysms), it is essential to consult a cardiologist to evaluate for myocarditis and possible aneurysm development.

A. This patient should be admitted for a complete evaluation.

B. This treatment plan is incomplete.

C. Although streptococcal pharyngitis and scarlet fever are in the differential, this plan does not address other diagnostic possibilities.

E. Cardiology should be notified and involved as early as possible when Kawasaki's disease is suspected, to assist with diagnosis, treatment, and long-term follow-up.

ANSWER 97

C. 4 years old. Gross motor skills at 4 years of age include hopping, skipping, and alternating feet going downstairs. Visual motor skills at 4 years of age include buttoning clothing fully and catching a ball. Language skills at 4 years of age include knowing colors, singing songs from memory. Social skills at 4 years of age include cooperative play.

A. 2-year-old infants are able to walk up and down stairs, but not hop, may remove pants and shoes, but does not exhibit fully developed language usage or parallel play.

B. 3-year-old infants may alternate feet going up steps, dress and undress partially, use 3-word sentences, and begin group play.

D. 5-year-old infants may skip alternating feet, tie shoes, print their first name, and play competitive games.

E. 6-year-old children are in kindergarten to 1st grade and know their ABCs, may count upto ten, form friendships, and do household chores.

ANSWER 98

E. Hand-foot-and-mouth disease is caused by coxsackie A viruses. As with most viral exanthems, the treatment is supportive care. Anorexia may develop due to the painful ulcers in the mouth. Fluids are encouraged to maintain hydration. Some physicians recommend a mouthwash made with Maalox or Kaopectate with diphenhyramine to control the pain before meals. Acetaminophen or ibuprofen may be used to treat the fever, which usually lasts about 2–3 days.

A. Paramyxovirus causes measles.

B. Rubella virus causes rubella.

C. Herpes virus 6 is associated with roseola infantum.

D. Erythema infectiosum, or fifth disease, is caused by parvovirus B-19.

ANSWER 99

D. This is ordinary "nursemaids elbow" which is a subluxation of the radial head. It is usually an innocent injury, commonly inflicted by lifting the child by one arm.

A. X-rays are usually not needed.

B. This diagnosis is rarely associated with child abuse.

C. Subluxation of the radial head is easily reduced by flexing the arm and the elbow and supinating the arm.

ANSWER 100

D. Hyponatremic dehydration occurs in about 20% of patients with dehydration. Symptomatic hyponatremia should be treated with 3% NaCl, until the symptoms resolve and the serum Na is elevated above 120.

A. Zinc deficiency is a chronic disorder with failure to thrive, hair loss, and dermatitis.

B. Presents at 1–2 years of age after the introduction of gluten in the diet.

C. Does not typically cause seizures.

E. Hypoglycemia, not hyperglycemia, may cause seizures.